HUSSAIN

and the

STRUGGLE

for

JUSTICE

HUSSAIN AND THE STRUGGLE FOR JUSTICE

The epic story of the grandson
of the Prophet Muhammad re-told
by a Christian theologian

CHRIS HEWER

Contemporary Thoughts Press

BRITISH LIBRARY CATALOGUING-IN-PUBLICATION DATA

A catalogue record for this book is available from the British Library.

ISBN: 978-1-914282-03-4

Production services by Advent Publishing Services, Leeds.

Contemporary Thoughts Press
71 Kendal Road, London NW10 1JE
Email: info@contemporarythoughtspress.com

Contents

About the Author

With a background in Christian theology, Islamic studies, education, and interfaith dialogue, the author of *Hussain and the Struggle for Justice* has for many years engaged with Muslims in the United Kingdom and around the world. A leading figure in Christian–Muslim relations in his home country since 1986, Dr Chris Hewer first worked at the Centre for the Study of Islam and Christian–Muslim Relations in Birmingham and then from 1999 to 2005 as the Adviser on Inter-Faith Relations to the Bishop of Birmingham. From 2006 to 2010, Dr Hewer was the St Ethelburga Fellow in Christian–Muslim Relations in London, connecting with a wide audience through the provision of adult popular education courses, study days, and public talks. He is currently involved in teaching, producing resource material, and writing.

In the
Name of God
the Compassionate
the Merciful

Publisher's Preface

In the Name of God, the Compassionate, the Merciful

Imam Hussain is an important figure in the history of Islam who has had a positive impact on Muslims over many centuries. The tragic martyrdom of the Imam has always been a strong source of inspiration for Muslims wherever they faced tyranny and oppression. It is one of the reasons, for example, why devout Muslims invoke blessings of peace upon Hussain on every mention of his name. The annual commemoration of the selfless sacrifice of Imam Hussain has spurred many Muslims to explore the wisdom of their faith and to live a life which accords with the noble tenets of Islam. It is important, therefore, to try to understand what Imam Hussain did throughout his life to maintain a true understanding of the faith established by his grandfather, the Prophet Muhammad.

A point came in the life of Imam Hussain where he found himself unable to obey the political ruler of his day, Yazid b. Mu'awiya, an unjust and profligate person who openly flouted the teachings of Islam and the tradition of the Prophet Muhammad. While Yazid presented himself as the caliph of the Islamic nation, his careless and immoral lifestyle was considered by many to make him unfit for leadership. It was Yazid who held power over the Islamic territories at the time of the Battle of Karbala in which Imam Hussain and seventy-two of his companions were brutally killed with the accompanying women and children taken captive.

Many Muslim scholars have attempted to answer 'what', 'how', and 'why' questions pertaining to the life of Imam Hussain. Non-Muslims have also over the centuries endeavoured to discover the meaning of Imam Hussain's life and death. Nevertheless, there remains a shortage of insightful perspectives written in English on the beacon of humanity that is Imam Hussain. To address this issue the Contemporary Thoughts Press cooperated with Dr Chris Hewer to write a book about Imam Hussain. Dr Hewer has extensive experience engaging with Muslims and has shown great interest in Imam Hussain's intellectual and moral heritage. I hope that the current book will help readers to appreciate Imam Hussain and to become better acquainted with not just his deeds and actions but also his spirit.

H.I.W.M. SEYED HASHEM MOOSAVI
Director of the Contemporary Thoughts Press

Introduction

Few people in world history have been so important
that their names have lived on for centuries. How
many events are of such significance that they are
commemorated every year by tens of millions? What
does it say when people are prepared to risk their
lives to be able to take part in such acts of remembrance? Such a person was Hussain, the grandson of
Muhammad, the Prophet of Islam. The event was the
terrible massacre in 680 when he was killed along with
seventy-two companions. Yet this event is thought of
as a victory. A victory for justice and truth. A victory
to show that the purity of the message brought by the
Qur'an and given to Muhammad must be defended
at all costs and not defiled by those not worthy of it.

Something had gone horribly wrong in the early
Muslim community. Here was the grandson of the
Prophet being killed by those who claimed to lead that
community, not even fifty years after Muhammad's
death. How could such a catastrophe happen? As

the grandson of Muhammad, who had been loved by his grandfather, who always wanted to have him nearby, all Muslims have great love and respect for Hussain. His killing is not a sectarian issue: one group of pious Muslims against another. It was the action of corrupt, tyrannical individuals who had captured the leadership of the Muslim community. Muslims, both Sunni and Shi'a, find that many of the leaders of this Umayyad dynasty, which ruled the Muslims from 661 to 750, were unworthy of that office and were far away from the ideals and practices of Islam as taught by the Qur'an and Muhammad.

The massacre took place on the tenth of the Muslim month of Muharram, the first month of the Muslim calendar, at a place called Karbala in Iraq. Shi'a Muslims, who have a special love for, and devotion to, Hussain (who has a unique and revered place in their understanding) will spend the first ten days of this month in deep mourning, remembering those events that culminated in the massacre. The beginning of the Islamic year is not just a season of mourning for Shi'a Muslims but also one of self-reflection and rededication – rededication of their lives to the ideals by which Hussain lived and for which he died. This period of revival comes to a climax on the tenth day, the anniversary of the massacre itself, the Day of Ashura. Throughout the world, wherever there are Shi'a Muslims, the Day of Ashura will be commemorated as a day of solemn lamentation. Ashura is followed by a period of forty days of subdued mourning, during which no weddings or other festivities take place. The whole season comes to an end on the fortieth day, Arbaeen, when millions of people converge on Karbala to pay their respects to Hussain and his stand for uprightness and justice. This pilgrimage to Karbala on Arbaeen goes way back into history; it commemorates the visit made forty days after the event by members of the family of Hussain who survived the massacre. At times of persecution pilgrims took back roads and travelled by night to avoid mortal danger. Many will walk fifty miles to Karbala from the city of Najaf, which is home to the shrine of Hussain's father. Others walk even greater distances from Iran or even from India. In recent years, the number of pilgrims has been approaching twenty million, making it the largest annual gathering on earth. It is a monumental achievement of the communities through which they pass, that the pilgrims are given food, drink, and first aid; places are found for them to rest and sleep. All in an atmosphere of peace and harmony.

The history of humankind has witnessed many tragedies; in this sense the massacre at Karbala is not unique. It shows us the depths to which human beings can sink. It shows us also the length to which people are capable of going for the sake of their high ideals, for the sake of the just cause in which they believe, and out of pure love and devotion to God. The martyrdom of Hussain and his companions stands head and shoulders above such tragedies in the history of Islam. We might reflect upon the status of Hussain, the devastation of his family, what would have happened if the stand had not been taken, and the brilliance of the beacon that was lit on that day to show a way for all men and women to follow. As the story unfolds, there is much here upon which we can all ponder.

As we might expect, the vast majority of those who make the Arbaeen walk are Shi'a Muslims, but Muslims of all traditions take part on this day. Not only Muslims, but people of other religions and people who belong to no faith community. A wide range of people have been inspired by the example of Hussain, from Gandhi to Martin Luther King and Nelson Mandela. It is a fundamental principle of religion that great religious figures do not belong to their own community alone but, because they belong to God, they belong to all humankind. Hussain, the hero of Karbala, is worthy of consideration by women and men of every age and place on earth – and that is the inspiration behind this short book.

It is hoped that this book will stimulate some discussion about the relevance of Hussain, and his grandfather, for our own times. Both Hussain and the Prophet Muhammad deserve to be better known and to be discussed by the widest possible audience. The story in these pages has been told using traditional Shi'a sources, as listed at the end of the book. Each chapter begins with some discussion points to draw out elements of what follows. All dates are given according to the Common Era. With profound thanks, I acknowledge the contribution of Shaykh Mohammad Saeed Bahmanpour, who read and commented on each chapter, helped to unpick knotty questions, and improved the translation of many quotations.

1.

WHO WAS HUSSAIN?

Every one of us is born into a certain context. We are born at a time and place, and into a certain family. Many of the influences of our early life just seem natural. What part did our parents play in shaping the way that we think and act? If we were lucky enough to know our grandparents, what part did they play in giving us a set of values, a way to live our lives? If you think back though, how much were you aware of this at the time? Often our characters are shaped before we really know what is happening to us. What must it be like though to be born into a particular role early in life? Maybe we were born into a farming family, when it was an automatic assumption that we would take over the family farm. Maybe we had parents who were doctors or teachers; naturally we would feel the call to follow them. As a great philosopher once said, 'Life can only be understood looking backwards, but it must be lived looking forwards.' To understand 'Who was Hussain?' we need to begin by looking at the family from which he came.

Hussain's grandfather was Muhammad, who was to become the Prophet of Islam. Muhammad was born in the year 570 CE into a family of merchants living in the city of Mecca in the Arabian Peninsula. As a young man, he learnt the family business and established a reputation for being trustworthy and honourable. Mecca was a city associated with Abraham. He and his son Ishmael had built there the Ka'bah, a simple cuboid building built for the worship of God alone. The Arabs of that area had followed the religion of Abraham and Ishmael. They came to the Ka'bah on pilgrimage to worship God. About four hundred years before the time of Muhammad, idol worship spread down to Mecca from the ancient civilisation around Syria. Muhammad came from a family who had never worshipped idols but believed that there is only one God. He was a religious seeker, always in search of deeper understanding of the one God in whom he believed.

By the time that he was twenty-five, Muhammad had established a reputation as a reliable and efficient merchant. He attracted the attention of a rich widow called Khadija. She had inherited her husband's business but looked for a manager to go on camel-train journeys carrying her merchandise to faraway markets. She employed Muhammad and was so impressed by his character that she asked him to marry her. They were in a monogamous marriage for twenty-five years until Khadija died.

Muhammad's uncle had a young son called Ali. He came to live with Muhammad and Khadija. He was an established member of the household and so his character was trained by them both. Muhammad, whose mission was to lead people back to the purity of the faith of Abraham, received his call to prophethood in the year 610 CE. This was when the Qur'an started to be revealed to him. It continued to be sent down from God in small portions until shortly before his death in 632 CE. For those not familiar with the contents of the Qur'an, Muslims believe it to be the last scripture sent by God to the earth that confirms earlier scriptures and corrects any errors that have crept into them over the centuries. It teaches the universal faith of Adam, Abraham, Moses, Jesus and thousands of other prophets sent by God to all the peoples of the earth. It contains guidance for an ethical way of life. Principal themes are the worship of God alone, establishing justice upon the earth, the value of all human life, the centrality of the family as the basis of society, care for the weak and defenceless, and that faith is expressed in actions to promote all that is good and oppose what is harmful within human society and the whole of creation.

Muhammad was told by God in the Qur'an to call a meeting of his family and to explain that he had been called to be a prophet of God. At this gathering Muhammad asked who would believe him and follow him. Only Ali came forward to pledge his belief and support. He was still a youth of nine years at this time but Muhammad declared that he would be his successor as head of the community after him.

Muhammad and Khadija were blessed with a daughter called Fatima. She too grew up in this household and so both she and Ali were able to observe the life of Muhammad at close quarters. The Qur'an says that Muhammad is a 'beautiful example' of the way in which a human life should be lived (Q. 33:21). This was a life lived in obedience to the message of the Qur'an. This would bring fulfilment in this life and lead one to the life of Paradise after death. Not surprisingly then, both Ali and Fatima had their characters shaped by the life and example of Muhammad. They noted what he said, the way in which he behaved and the way that he treated other people: they just 'drank in' the way of life that he lived. Ali knew from the beginning that he would be called to be the leader of the new Muslim community after Muhammad. Naturally, he modelled his whole life on the example that he received so that he could fulfil this calling.

When Fatima grew up and became a young woman, many men approached Muhammad to enquire if they might be able to marry her but it was always planned

4

in Muhammad's mind that Fatima should marry Ali, which she did. In this way they would carry on the style of life, shaped by the Qur'an and the example of Muhammad, into the next generation. Fatima and Ali had two sons, Hasan, who was born in 625 CE, and Hussain, who was born in 626 CE. As was the Arab custom, they both had 'son of Ali' included with their given name; so, Hussain ibn Ali. Khadija had died in 619 CE. The Household of the Prophet, or in Arabic the Ahl al-Bayt, then comprised five people: Muhammad, Ali, Fatima, Hasan and Hussain. Muhammad had a particular love for Fatima and always treated her with great respect. It is reported that he would stand up when she came into a gathering and give her his place. This special closeness continued throughout her life. We are told that when Muhammad lay dying, he told Fatima that his death was close. Her eyes were filled with tears. And then he told her that she would be the first of his family to die after him. And now her face was a picture of joy; to think that she would not have to live long without her beloved father and would soon join him in the life of Paradise.

There are many accounts of the special relationship that Muhammad had with his two grandchildren. As was quite common in Arab society at that time, he always spoke of them as his sons. He liked to have them near him as often as possible. We hear of him pausing a meeting when the two boys appeared and then bringing them to sit one on each knee. On one occasion, we are told that one or both of them climbed onto his shoulders while he was in prostration on the floor in prayer. He held onto them and allowed them to ride on his back as he completed the prayer. Although they were still small boys, everyone could notice the special rapport that they had with Muhammad and the way in which he would train their characters. Muhammad referred to them as 'The Leaders of the Youths of Paradise'.

Two special events made it very clear to Hasan and Hussain that they were indeed destined for a particular place within the Muslim community. Muslim scholars agree that these two events happened close together and towards the end of Muhammad's life. The first event is recorded in the Qur'an (Q. 33:33) in which, Fatima, Ali, Hasan and Hussain were called by the Prophet, who then covered them all with his cloak or blanket. It was on this occasion that the verse of the Qur'an was revealed, 'Indeed God desires to repel all impurity from you, O People of the Household [Ahl al-Bayt], and purify you with a thorough purification.' This event is of great importance especially for Shi'a Muslims. They understand that only the ultimately pure God can purify to an ultimate degree and thus these five, the Ahl al-Bayt, were rendered utterly pure and sinless. Therefore, when they spoke, their words could be relied upon to be without error. Over the next two hundred and fifty years, there were to be a further nine descendants of Hussain, who were chosen and similarly purified. These nine, plus Ali, Hasan and Hussain were the twelve divinely-appointed Imams, chosen by God to guide the community after the death of Muhammad. These twelve, plus Muhammad and his daughter, Fatima, exclusively comprise the fourteen members of the Ahl al-Bayt. Shi'a Muslims give particular weight to a Hadith, or authentic saying of Muhammad, that he would leave after him 'two most precious things', these being the Qur'an and the Ahl al-Bayt: never would they separate until the Day of Judgement at the end of the world. In this way, these divinely inspired leaders have an essential role to play as guardians of the authentic interpretation of Islam through all ages.

The second event took place in the year 631 CE, the year before Muhammad died. A delegation had come to visit him from a Christian settlement in the south of the Arabian Peninsula called Najran. They had a long and detailed discussion with Muhammad about the correct way to believe in and worship God and about the person of Jesus. It was on this occasion that a large portion of verses of the Qur'an were revealed (Q. 3:1–85). In these verses the Christian understanding of Jesus as a divine being was corrected; Jesus had the great honour of being a prophet of God, like Muhammad. No greater honour could be given to any human being but he was not divine. After long discussion, the Christians and Muhammad were unable to come to an agreement on this question.

It was then that Muhammad received a verse of the Qur'an which gave a way of resolving this question. 'Come! Let us call our sons and your sons, our women and your women, our souls and your souls, then let us pray earnestly and call down God's curse upon the liars' (Q. 3:61). This form of mutual cursing was known before in the biblical tradition (1 Kings 18:20–40). It was the ultimate way of resolving a question of great importance and allowing God to decide. Whoever was not telling the truth would be cursed, indeed killed, by God. In Arabic this was called *mubahala*.

The next morning the Muslim and the Christian groups were to send forward the people referred to in this verse and then pray for God ultimately to decide their dispute. Muhammad appeared with his daughter, Fatima (our women), Ali, whom Muhammad often referred to as his soul (*nafs*), and Hasan and Hussain (our sons). It is reported that when the Christian delegation saw the eminence of those who were standing against them and when they reflected that Muhammad was so certain of the truth of his position before God that he was prepared to stake his entire family on the question, they decided not to go through with the mutual cursing. They argued that if Muhammad was indeed a prophet of God, then no good could come from such a challenge. Instead they asked Muhammad to send a wise member of his community to live amongst them to act as a judge in any question that they could not resolve themselves. They agreed that they would go back to Najran and live under Muhammad's protection, for which they would make a contribution to the Muslim community treasury.

These two experiences, coming on top of all that they had heard from their parents and grandfather about their special position within the Muslim community, had a profound influence on Hasan and Hussain. They knew that they were called perfectly to obey God in all things and to be God's representatives in guiding the community after Muhammad's death. In this way their characters were formed during these early years. The experience of Muhammad having complete trust in God and being prepared to sacrifice himself and all his family for the sake of the message became a model for Hussain's later life as we shall see. Hasan was only eight-years-old and Hussain six-years-old when their grandfather Muhammad died. Their mother Fatima died shortly afterwards. From now on they would be trained in the way of life laid down by the Qur'an and the Prophet through the life and teaching of their father Ali.

2.

GROWING TO MATURITY

It is one thing to know that we are in the right but what do we do when things do not work out the way that we know they ought? This can be a test of character: do we keep going, or do we give up? Influence and power are not the same thing; which is the most productive? Even if we know that we should have power, but we don't, does this stop us having influence? What do we finally do when we have power: how do we react? How hard it can be to break away from the traditions that have always ruled our communities!

The great influence in the lives of Hasan and Hussain while growing up was their father, Ali. He was born in the year 601 CE. His father was the uncle of Muhammad and when he was five-years-old, he went to live with Muhammad and his wife Khadija. When the revelation of the Qur'an began, he pledged his allegiance to Muhammad as a young boy of nine-years-old. From that time onwards, he was the constant companion of Muhammad learning from him the way of Islam. During the years from 610 CE to 622 CE, the infant Muslim community in Mecca was under persecution. This was a testing time. Ali learnt by observing Muhammad how to persevere with patience and courage when things did not go the way that they ought. As a young man, Ali did not lack courage. When Muhammad and the Muslim community migrated from Mecca to Medina in 622 CE, Muhammad left Ali behind as his trusted representative. Although they persecuted him, people in Mecca knew that Muhammad was a man of honour, who could be trusted. They would leave their precious belongings in his safekeeping. Muhammad asked Ali to remain in Mecca until all these precious things were returned to their rightful owners; only then was he to make his own migration to Medina. At the time when Muhammad himself left for Medina, Ali slept in the place where Muhammad normally slept because they knew that an assassination attempt was planned. By sleeping in Muhammad's place, he gave him the opportunity of slipping away at night and thus fooling the assassins.

During the years in Medina, Ali was always active serving the community. He was a noted warrior: often, according to the practice of those times, he would be sent out to engage in single-handed combat with the champion of the armies from Mecca, who came to destroy Muhammad and his Muslim community. By engaging in such single-handed combat, the weight of saving the Muslim community from further attack and bloodshed rested upon the young Ali. He placed his trust in God and was always victorious. Ali was given the responsibility of being one of the official scribes to take down in writing the verses of the Qur'an as they were revealed. In this way he had direct access to Muhammad, who would explain to him alone both the outer and the hidden meaning of each verse. This allowed Ali to have a profound knowledge of the way of Islam, which meant that he was respected by the whole community for his wisdom and wise counsel. He often served as the representative of Muhammad, both in formal matters and in distributing charity. It was reported that he would go at night with a sackful of bread to deliver it unseen to those who were in need.

Although he knew that he had been designated as the divinely-appointed successor to Muhammad, this was not the way that things worked out. Immediately after Muhammad's death, it was Ali's responsibility to prepare his body for burial and arrange the funeral. During this time a group of the traditional tribal elders in the community gathered together and decided that another companion of Muhammad should become the head of the community. Although

Ali and his followers pointed out that this was not the way that things should be, Ali did not press his claim. He knew that this would lead to a dispute within the community, which would result in bloodshed and he wanted to avoid this. From 632 CE when Muhammad died until 656 CE, Ali saw three other men chosen within the community to take on the role of leader or caliph. During this time Ali served as a wise counsellor and a source of spiritual guidance to members of the community. In this way he exercised a profound influence in the lives of many.

During the time of the third of these leaders, Uthman, a degree of corruption set in within the Muslim community. He had chosen to appoint members of his own family to positions of power, thus giving them access to wealth as the Muslim community expanded. Ultimately, this led to the assassination of Uthman by a disgruntled group of the companions of Muhammad, who had come to complain about their grievances under the governor of Egypt. It was at this time that the Muslim community turned to Ali, in 656 CE, to become the caliph. One of those family members that Uthman had appointed to be the governor of Syria was a man called Mu'awiya. He was of the opinion that Ali had not sufficiently pursued the assassins to avenge the death of Uthman. He refused to pledge allegiance to Ali on this account.

Now that Ali had political power, he set about removing those people who had been unworthy of the positions that had been given to them. He wanted to root out all forms of financial corruption. His plan was to restore the Muslim community to the original purity of the message contained in the Qur'an as implemented by Muhammad. He wanted to make sure that everyone within the community was treated equally and gave particular attention to relieving the poverty of the poor and orphans. Mu'awiya became the leader of the group who opposed Ali and this almost led to civil war within the community. There were some battles between the forces of Mu'awiya and those of Ali, but he sought to negotiate so as to avoid wholesale bloodshed. This did not please all those who were willing to fight with him and eventually one of these people assassinated Ali in 661 CE.

Before his death, Ali nominated his elder son, Hasan, to succeed him as head of the community or, as the Shi'a call him, the Imam. This was not acceptable to Mu'awiya, who retained his power base in Syria and wanted to establish his own dynasty, the Umayyads. Mu'awiya had a strong military force and made an alliance with governors of other provinces. If Imam Hasan had called the community to arms to oppose Mu'awiya, there would have been great loss of life. Hasan decided that the wise course of action, for the sake of the innocent members of the community, was to agree to give up political power and retain his position as spiritual guide and wise counsellor.

3.

LEADERSHIP WITHOUT POLITICAL POWER

It's a sad reality of life. Once the bully gains the upper hand, once the dictator has power, many people start to believe in the propaganda that is put out. We have seen it in the twentieth century: how could people in the European dictatorships have been taken in? They had centuries of civilisation behind them. Most people just went with the flow. How does the just man or woman, the leader, react? What is it to live in a society ruled by values with which one does not agree? Does one have to accept those values? What about if one regards those values as wrong and indeed evil, even though they are dressed up to deceive and appear to be good and righteous? Is it enough to keep oneself free and untainted? 'To live in the world but not to accept its values.' There can be wisdom in this. But what about when one is a leader, when other people look to you for guidance and to set an example? What then is the correct response?

~

During the last terminal illness of Prophet Muhammad, his daughter Fatima brought his two grandsons, Hasan and Hussain, to him and asked Muhammad to give them an inheritance. He did not have any material wealth to leave them, but to Hasan, he said, 'I give you my form and my nobility.' To Hussain, he said, 'I give you my generosity and my bravery.' The nobility of Hasan shone through the period of his life after the death of his father, Ali, right up until his own death. He was designated by his father to take over the leadership of the community. But from the outset, Mu'awiya, the governor of Syria, was opposed to him, as he had been opposed to his father, Ali, and wanted to find ways to undermine his administration. He sent out spies to keep him informed of Hasan's actions and to sow dissent within the community.

There was bound to be an animosity between Mu'awiya and the Ahl al-Bayt. Mu'awiya and his father and mother's family had opposed Muhammad and the Muslim community from their base in Mecca. They had fought in the Meccan armies against the Muslims. Their embrace of Islam only occurred when the city of Mecca had fallen to the Muslims just two years before Muhammad's death. Mu'awiya was of the same tribe as Uthman, the third caliph, therefore he was angry when he thought that Hasan's father, Ali, had not sufficiently avenged his death. It was the Ahl al-Bayt that stood in the way of him establishing the Umayyad dynasty and thus entrenching his family's powerbase for the future.

Hasan wanted to preserve the unity of the Muslim community if possible. There were many people within the community who were committed to waging war with Mu'awiya for a whole host of reasons of their own. Some of these even attacked Hasan when he refused to declare an all-out battle. Struggling for political power was not Hasan's primary concern. He wanted to guide the community according to the values and way of life laid out by the Qur'an and his grandfather Muhammad. Having political power could contribute to this end, but power was not the goal in itself. He knew that Mu'awiya was using bribery to increase his power base and to build up sufficient force to overthrow Hasan when he chose. Hasan knew that even those who loudly pledged their support for him and their willingness to fight might well desert him if it came to battle.

Rather than fight against the forces of Mu'awiya, which would mean huge loss of life and the shedding of much Muslim blood, Hasan decided to enter into negotiation with Mu'awiya. A treaty was proposed by Mu'awiya and jointly drawn up. If Mu'awiya would agree to this treaty, then Hasan would agree to withdraw from political power and public life, and to concentrate on the spiritual development of the community. The terms of this treaty emphasised the need for peace and security for the whole Muslim community. The teaching of the Qur'an and the practice of Muhammad should form the basis for law within the community. The practice that had been promoted by Mu'awiya and some of his followers of publicly cursing Hasan's father, Ali, had to stop. Those people within the community who had supported Ali and Hasan were to have their rights respected and they were not to be persecuted. Prisoners were to be released. Mu'awiya agreed that he would not appoint a successor but would leave the question to be decided by the Muslim community.

The treaty was agreed by both sides and Hasan withdrew to live quietly in Medina. Mu'awiya went immediately to Iraq and cynically asserted that his triumph over Hasan was for power over the people and not for their welfare or to promote their practice of Islam. He made it clear that he had no intention of upholding the terms of the treaty and the practice of cursing the name of Ali in public gatherings continued. Back in Medina, Hasan was not idle. He wanted to consolidate the goodness and virtue of the people. Had it come to fighting, many good people would have died, instead he wanted to work with these good people to solidify their grasp of Islamic values and thus to improve the society for the sake of everyone. Hasan was not opposed to the use of force as such, especially when he learned that Mu'awiya had only contempt for the terms of the treaty that they had signed, but he knew that the time was not right. He was in Medina 'waiting on God's command' for the right time to act. He summed up his position by saying, 'I have entered into a truce to avoid bloodshed and out of consideration for myself, my family, and my dedicated companions.'

Some of the key elements in the spiritual teaching of Hasan during this time emphasised contemplating the inevitability of death, stressing that it was not something that any of us could ultimately avoid. He counselled people to stay active in the affairs of the world in which they lived and to engage as though they would live forever, but at the same time to abstain from worldly ambitions, as if they might die tomorrow. As far as wealth is concerned, he advised people not to accumulate more than they would need to survive. They were to remember that everyone will have to give an account before God of the legitimacy of all their earnings. Twice in his life, he gave away all his wealth to the poor, and three times, he divided what he had and gave one half to those in need. The highest dignity towards which people should strive and for which they should be honoured was to be obedient to God in all things. Finally, he advised people to seek the company of wise men and women who would appreciate the good in them and who would also correct any failings in their character.

Hussain was active in the support of his brother and was likewise urging people towards the higher values of Islam. We may take just one example of his spiritual teaching, patience and wisdom. A man entered Medina who was notorious for his hatred of Hussain's father, Ali. As soon as he saw Hussain he began to abuse him and to speak badly of both him and his father. Hussain remained calm and waited until he had finished. Then Hussain responded by quoting some verses from the Qur'an: 'Adopt a policy of excusing the faults of people, bid what is right, and turn away from the ignorant. Should a temptation from Satan disturb you, invoke the protection of God, indeed he is the all-hearing, all-knowing. When those who are God-conscious are touched by a visitation of Satan they remember God and, behold, they perceive. But their brethren, they draw them into error and then they do not spare any harm' (Q. 7:199–202). Then Hussain said to the man, 'You have been misled. Take it easy. Pray for our and your forgiveness from God. If you need our help, then we are willing to help. If you need our protection, then we are willing to defend you. And if you need our guidance, then we are willing to guide you.' At this the man was very ashamed of his rude remarks, especially when Hussain repeated to him the words that Joseph had spoken to his brothers when he met them in Egypt, 'From today onwards, there shall be no blame on you. May God forgive you and he is the most merciful' (Q. 12:92). Hussain then told the man that he should ask him for whatever he needed. The man commented, 'When I heard this, I felt so ashamed but could not find any place to hide myself. Moreover, I wished the earth would tear apart and I would fall into it. After this encounter there is no-one on the face of this earth who is more beloved to me than Imam Hussain and his father, Imam Ali.'

We can appreciate something of the character of Hussain by some of the short sayings of his that have been preserved for us.

Be steadfast and firm in the way towards what is right, even if your journey is full of pain and challenges.

By God, I will never surrender to my enemies like a humiliated person and never pledge allegiance to them like slaves.

To me, death for the sake of what is right, is nothing but happiness, and living under tyrants nothing but living in hell.

The most generous person is the one who gives to those who do not expect his help.

People are slaves of this world. Religion is just what they say. They use it as long as it provides them with their living. When they are tested, there remain only a few true religious ones.

If you don't believe in any religion, at least be free-spirited and honest in your actions.

God will help the person who cares about other people's needs, both in this world and the hereafter.

Beware! Do not be among those who are concerned about the sins of others while neglectful of their own sins.

One who reveals your faults to you like a mirror is your true friend, and one who flatters you and covers up your faults is your enemy.

Kindness elevates human beings, and faithfulness is a sign of decency.

One of the signs of a scholar is criticising his or her own words and thoughts and being aware of different viewpoints.

During the years that Hussain lived in Medina, he married several times. Sometimes his wife died when she was still young and then he married another. In total there were five wives, who each bore him children. This means that some of his sons and daughters had different mothers. We will go through the list of mothers and children, including the probable dates of birth of the children and their ages in 680 CE, when the events of Karbala took place. His first wife was Rubab, who was the only wife to be present on the day of the massacre itself. She was the mother of a girl, called Sukayna (sometimes also written as Sakina) who was born in 667 CE, and a boy called Abdullah Ali Asghar, who was born in 680 CE. His second wife was Layla, who bore him his first child, a boy called Ali Akbar, in 653 CE. His third wife was Shahrbanu, a Persian lady, who was the daughter of Yazdegerd, the last Sassanid king of Persia, who gave birth to Ali ibn Hussain in 656 CE. He was to succeed Hussain as the fourth Imam according to Shi'a understanding, and was known as Imam Zayn al-Abidin ('The Adornment of the Worshippers'), which is the name we will use for him from now on. His fourth wife was called Umm Ishaq and she had a daughter in 671 CE, who was called Fatima al-Sughra. Finally, there was another wife, whose name has not been recorded but who was from the tribe of Qada'ah. She too had a son called Ja'far but both mother and son had died by the time of the battle at Karbala. All five of the surviving children of Hussain were present at Karbala. Their probable ages at this time were: Ali Akbar, twenty-seven; Zayn al-Abidin, twenty-five; Sukayna, fourteen; Fatima al-Sughra, nine; and Abdullah Ali Asghar, six months.

In the year 669 CE, Hasan was poisoned. It seems

highly likely that this was done on the orders of Mu'awiya so that he could open the way to appoint his son, Yazid, as his successor. Hasan knew that he had been poisoned; it took him some time to die. He summoned his brother Hussain, designated him as his successor, and gave him instructions about his inheritance. He gave orders that whoever had been responsible for poisoning him should not be pursued; the punishment should be left to God. He strictly forbade any fighting concerning his death or the place at which he was to be buried. He asked that on the way to his burial he should be taken to the grave of his grandfather Muhammad, so that he might bid him farewell. After he had died, Hussain prepared his brother's body for burial, and then had him carried to the grave of Muhammad. There was opposition from some people, thinking that there was a plan to bury him alongside his grandfather, but Hussain quieted them by telling them that was not their plan. Hasan had asked that he should be buried in the cemetery of al-Baqi in Medina close to the grave of Fatima bint Asad, the mother of his father, Ali. This is where his grave can be found today, although the mausoleum that stood there for centuries was destroyed in 1925 by the Wahhabis when they came to power.

4.

'MY WORD IS MY BOND'

Do you remember a time when deals were struck by two people shaking hands? Since 1801 the motto of the London Stock Exchange has been 'my word is my bond'. If two people made an agreement verbally then that was the end of the matter. Both could rely on the other. I wonder if it always worked like that in practice. It relies on both partners to the deal being people of good faith who will hold firm to their agreement. If one person is untrue then the whole deal collapses. What does the person of integrity do then? Can one person be bound by a promise made by someone else?

∽

At the death of Hasan, Hussain became the Imam, the spiritual head of the community charged to lead

the people and guide them according to the original
message set out in the Qur'an and put into practice
by the Prophet Muhammad. This was not all that he
inherited. He took over the treaty made between his
brother Hasan and Mu'awiya. In Shi'a Muslim understanding, the Ahl al-Bayt were rendered pure and
sinless, therefore when they spoke, they did so without
error. This means that when Hasan had entered into
that treaty, he was acting under the inspiration of God.
Hussain made it clear that he would remain true to
the treaty undertaken by his brother, provided that
the treaty was not broken by Mu'awiya.

Hussain continued to live a withdrawn life in
Medina guiding and inspiring all those members of
the Muslim community who looked to him. Although
he did not feel that the time was right to press his
claim to leadership, he did not shrink back from
drawing attention to the failings and wrongdoings
of Mu'awiya. Hussain was convinced of the rightness
of his cause and so was not moved by, or afraid of,
the words or actions of Mu'awiya. Mu'awiya was not
pleased to be corrected in this way. But he held the
reins of power and so felt that he could not be touched
by an armed uprising. He also controlled the treasury
of the Muslim community, which meant that he could
use bribery to coerce people to do his bidding. This
was a time of expansion for the Muslim empire and
as more territory came under their control so more
money flowed into the central treasury. Many people

were simply prepared to go along with the rule of Mu'awiya, either through fear or because they could gain personally by such association.

A story is told from this time which will illustrate the different approaches of Hussain and Mu'awiya. A letter was sent by Mu'awiya to the governor of Medina instructing him to ask for the hand of Umm Kulthoom, the daughter of Zaynab, Hussain's sister, to be married to Yazid, the son of Mu'awiya. He said that he would be willing to offer any dowry that was asked for by the girl's father and that he would pay all her father's debts. Such a marriage, he said, would serve to bind together the family of Muhammad and the Umayyad clan. The young woman's father, who had amassed considerable debts through his generosity to others, said that the decision about whom she should marry should be made by Hussain. The governor approached Hussain and repeated the proposal to him. Hussain said that the proposal should be made in a public assembly comprising members of both families. The governor stood in the assembly, praised God, and then repeated the proposal before all assembled. He then spoke to Hussain directly. He said that for Hussain and his family to be associated with the son of Mu'awiya, and therefore the Umayyads, would be a great honour for Hussain. He said that Yazid had no equal in status and that the rain from heaven falls as a blessing for his face (soul).

Hussain rose and gave praises to God. He said that

it was the custom of Muhammad himself to give a dowry of no more than 480 dirhams (about enough to buy five camels). This then was the customary dowry for all members of the Prophet's family. A dirham was a small silver coin. Hussain said that it would not be fitting that the family's debts should be offset as part of the marriage agreement for one of their daughters. Further, he said, the disagreement between the two families was a matter concerning obedience to God and not something that could be reconciled by money or a marriage. He took grave exception to the suggestion that the family of Muhammad should find any honour by association with Yazid, the son of Mu'awiya. On the contrary, any honour would flow the other way round. Finally, the only person worthy to claim the blessing of rain from the heavens was Prophet Muhammad himself. Hussain then announced to the whole assembly that Umm Kulthoom should be betrothed in marriage to her cousin Qasim. The dowry should be as the Prophet decreed, 480 dirhams. Hussain then proceeded to give the couple a piece of land, the proceeds of which would be more than 80,000 dirhams per year, which would provide them with a living.

Hussain had supporters outside the city of Medina. The city of Kufa in Iraq, which had been the power base of his father Ali, and in which he had been killed, contained many who recognised Hussain as the rightful head of the community. Some of their leaders wrote letters to Hussain pleading with him to rise up, attack and defeat Mu'awiya. They said that they would support him and stand with him in the battle. Hussain's response was always to write back and tell them to stay at home. He was not prepared to be the one who would break the treaty that his brother had signed with Mu'awiya.

It was Mu'awiya himself who had broken the treaty throughout. Finally, he decided to nominate his son, Yazid, as his successor. That action violated the most important part of the treaty and therefore Hussain no longer felt himself bound by it. When Mu'awiya died in 680 CE and Yazid took power and began to consolidate his position, the die was cast for confrontation with Hussain.

5.

LEADERSHIP IN THE FACE OF TYRANNY

Whether in business or in politics, how often have we looked at someone and asked, 'How on earth did you get the position that you have?' The awful reality is, if one is prepared to use brute force and bribery, or to tell plausible lies, then the incompetent bully can often come out on top; at least for a period of time. The one in charge is supposed to promote justice, to fight oppression and to ensure the well-being of all; but what about when those in charge are corrupt? We don't need iron chains to turn people into slaves; putting people in your debt means that you can control them. When faced with tyranny the hard question is when to compromise and when to make a stand.

The Bible records a time of tyranny (2 Maccabees

6:18–31). Jerusalem was under occupation. The tyrants wanted to force people to abandon their religion and to worship alien gods. They brought out one of the respected elders of the community in front of the assembled people. Eleazar was a man of 90 years, respected for his piety and learning. He was to be forced to eat pork that had been sacrificed to idols. If he would do it, then everyone would follow his example. His oppressors offered to secretly bring him kosher meat that he could eat; nobody else would know, they would all think that he had betrayed his faith and do likewise. His answer was clear and determined. 'Should I allow the people to think that I would abandon my faith for the sake of another couple of years of life? I fear God more than you.' He walked boldly to the torture block where they beat him to death with clubs.

In 676 CE, Mu'awiya formally and publicly named his son, Yazid, as his successor. By doing so he violated the treaty that he had made with Hasan and which had been kept faithfully by Hussain. This was bound to lead to confrontation between Hussain and Mu'awiya. Mu'awiya knew that he was on a weak foundation with the people, so he sought to stabilise his position by putting pressure on provincial governors and other people of influence in the community to accept his

nomination and support Yazid. Hussain and some other leading members of his extended family refused to give their backing to someone that they knew was quite unworthy of the office.

According to the treaty with Hasan, the question of the succession should have been resolved by the Muslim community itself. One way that this might have happened would have been through a council of the most senior leaders within the community. Hussain and those who stood with him against this nomination would likely be members of such a council. In his terminal illness, Mu'awiya summoned his son Yazid and spoke to him about Hussain and the others that he thought might oppose his succession. Part of what he said is recorded: 'As far as Hussain ibn Ali is concerned, he is an insignificant man, and I hope that God would protect you from him by means of those who killed his father and deserted his brother. He has close kinship, a great claim, and is a relation of Muhammad. I don't think the people of Iraq would leave him alone until they make him a rebel. If you should overpower him, pardon him, for if I were his master, I would pardon him.' Even Mu'awiya, who had no liking or respect for Hussain, would not have killed him on account of his being the grandson of Muhammad. He is reported to have made it plain to Yazid, in this terminal phase of his life, that Hussain would never pledge allegiance to him, so he ought not to press for it.

Mu'awiya died during April 680 CE. Yazid was not present at his death or for his burial. When he arrived, he went to the grave to pay his respects. Then on 22 April 680 CE, he was sworn in as the new caliph. His first thought was to consolidate his power by demanding an oath of allegiance from all the people of influence in the community. He wrote to the governor of Medina and ordered that he was to seize Hussain and two others whom he feared would publicly oppose him. The governor was ordered to demand the oath of allegiance. He was commanded to act so fiercely that they would have no chance to do anything before giving the oath. The penalty for refusing to give the oath was death.

For Shi'a Muslims, Yazid is the greatest of all tyrants, for he is the one who would command the martyrdom of Hussain and seventy-two of his faithful companions, as well as the capture and degradation of the surviving women and children of his party. Yazid was notorious for loose living, corruption regarding the public funds and appointments to public office, and his disregard for the teachings of the Qur'an and Prophet Muhammad. There are even reports of him denying the validity of these two most fundamental foundations of the religion of Islam. Sunni Muslim sources are also damning of Yazid's character. The great Sunni scholar, Ibn Khaldun, wrote of his 'corruption and evil'. The monumental Sunni historian and commentator on the Qur'an, al-Tabari, wrote of his devotion to hunting, an easy-going life and his neglect of the teachings of Islam. He records that Yazid's own advisers counselled him to change his behaviour before he took office.

From the time that Yazid took power, the die was cast as regards to an ultimate confrontation with Hussain. Like all bullies and dictators, Yazid was morally weak and could not tolerate opposition leaders within the community, who could become the focus for rebellion against his rule. He could not back off from such a confrontation or else he would lose everything. The choice for Hussain was stark and clear, take the oath of allegiance to him or face death. The eyes of the Muslim community would be on Hussain to see if he would give in and take the oath. If he did so, then it would mean that they could all do so also. The moment for decisive leadership had come.

Faith is not a matter of intellectual assent: just to say, 'I believe' is not enough. Even Satan believes in the existence of God! Faith demands action; not 'I believe' but 'I do. I obey God's commands. I express my belief through my deeds.' An incident that illustrates this truth is reported from the life of Muhammad, when he was old and weakened through illness towards the end of his life. He was being helped by his companions to come to the mosque to join the congregational prayer. Some men from the community, moved with compassion for his condition, no doubt, suggested to him that he could be excused joining the prayers on this occasion. His response was emphatic. 'Yes, even me. Until your very last breath keep on doing what is right and avoiding the temptation to take the easy option. We live the whole of our life in the tension between hope in the mercy of God and fear of divine retribution.' Hussain must have had to the forefront of his mind a saying reported from his grandfather, Muhammad, 'The greatest jihad is to speak a word of truth into the face of the tyrant.'

What would be the consequences of Hussain giving in and accepting the authority of Yazid? It would not only be opening the door to corruption, to the exploitation of members of the Muslim community and to endorsing tyrannical rule. It would also mean that the drift away from the purity of the authentic teaching of the Qur'an and Prophet Muhammad that had already taken place would turn into a flood. It was not an individual's pride that was at stake. It was not even the sense that the rightful leader of the community had been deprived of that position. For Hussain and for Shi'a Muslims in later generations, what was at stake was the very message of Islam itself, the way of life decreed by God that would bring those who followed it to justice and peace in this life and lead people to find favour with God and enter paradise after death. The stakes could not be higher.

6.

THE SANCTITY OF HUMAN LIFE

Can you think of any act more serious than taking the life of another human being? How heavy must the decision be to engage in such an action! Islam teaches that every human life is of infinite value. How can we engage in fighting if we value the human life of every single member of the enemy just as much as we value our own? If we think back in our own history, we can see times when there has been a tendency to rush into battle. Is it cowardice to seek to avoid bloodshed if at all possible? Are there limits that cannot be crossed? When do we reach the point at which there seems to be no alternative but to fight?

During one of the Sikh wars in 1704, there was a water-carrier called Bhai Kanhaiya. He would have a skin of water slung over his back and his job would be to go to the sick and wounded to ease their suffering with a drink of water. His own comrades noticed that he was giving water to the injured of both sides. They complained to their leader, Guru Gobind Singh, who sent for the water-carrier. When Bhai Kanhaiya was questioned, he admitted freely that he had tended the wounded on both sides. He explained: 'I saw only suffering human beings.' The Guru commended his action, told him to continue, and gave him bandages and ointment so that he could better ease the suffering of all these human beings.

Once Hussain knew that the agent of Yazid was commanded to come to him and demand that he take the oath of allegiance, he had a real question to resolve. He knew that Yazid had a powerful army behind him and that he was ruthless. Yazid could not afford to back down and therefore he would fight. Any battle with such a powerful army would result in massive loss of life. Hussain also knew that if he called people to arms, in order to defend the rightness of his cause, then a large number of people would respond. The result would be great numbers of Muslim dead. Many would be wounded and thus men would be incapable of providing for their families. This meant huge numbers of Muslim widows and orphans. This would be one of those most awful wars, a civil war, brother against brother, Muslims dead and crippled on both sides. Could that be avoided?

Surely, Hussain must have reflected on the situation when his own brother Hasan had seen Mu'awiya seize power at the death of their father, Ali. Hasan faced a similar problem: if he had called men to arms to oppose Mu'awiya, Muslim blood would have been spilt on both sides. Given the size and experience in battle of Mu'awiya's army, it was highly likely that the victory would have been theirs. Hasan knew as well that some of those who would have come to respond to his call would not remain when the going got tough and would withdraw and go home. Considering all the circumstances, Hasan decided to make the treaty with Mu'awiya. If he himself survived, then the message of the true interpretation of Islam would also survive. He could build up the faith and understanding of those who looked to him for spiritual leadership. In this way, the message would live on in their lives. Even though it must have caused Hasan great pain to make that treaty, and to see the way in which Mu'awiya conducted himself in power, it was the right course, the most courageous thing to do.

Hussain's own father, Ali, was a noted warrior, a veteran of many battles. He was faced with a similar problem at the death of Muhammad. He knew that he had been designated by God and the Prophet to lead the community after Muhammad's death. Yet the community chose another path. Instead of calling his men to arms and engaging in a civil war with other Muslims, the companions of Muhammad himself, he decided to make his position clear in speech and then withdraw. Again, he was inspired by the value of every human life and wished to avoid bloodshed if possible; even to his own disadvantage. He also worked for the good of the community out of the limelight, where he could build them up to be true to the message of Islam.

On two further occasions in the life of Ali, we can see this same desire to spare bloodshed if at all possible. When he encountered the army of Mu'awiya at the Battle of Siffin in 657 CE, faced with many deaths on both sides, he agreed to go to arbitration. Even though he was betrayed and tricked by the agents of Mu'awiya, he held his resolve and remained true to his word. Some groups amongst his soldiers vehemently disagreed with his position and saw it as a lack of faith in God, because if they had faith and were in the right, then God would have granted them victory. They left his side and went away. Eventually, it was one of these who assassinated Ali in 661 CE. Again, we see his character. As he lay dying, he instructed that there should be no fighting or reprisals on account of his assassination. Only the assassin himself should be brought to justice.

Hussain must have heard reports of an incident in the life of Muhammad himself that happened when Hussain was only a small boy. Muhammad had seen in a dream that he was to make a visit to the city of Mecca as a pilgrimage to worship God at the Ka'bah, where his ancestor Abraham had worshipped. Abraham and Ishmael had built the Ka'bah, and then gone around and around it calling out the praises of God. When the Muslims of Medina knew that this was the Prophet's intention, they were delighted and resolved to join him in the pilgrimage. It was the right of all Arabs who came as pilgrims to enter Mecca, so this was something of a test. They had a great love for the pilgrimage city, even though it was presently forbidden to them because it was still in the hands of idol-worshippers, the seat of the enemy, who had fought them in three battles. They were all dressed as pilgrims, which meant that they bore no fighting weapons, and had made the intention to observe peace throughout.

It is reported that around 1,400 Muslims went with Muhammad towards Mecca. A delegation from Mecca came out to meet them at a place called Hudaibiyya. The Muslims were told that the Meccans would not allow them to enter the city. The Meccans went home that night and were to return in the morning for further discussions. It is reported that Muhammad went throughout his camp during the night taking a solemn promise from all his companions that they would obey him in the morning whatever he commanded. In the morning when negotiations resumed, Muhammad gave way to the Meccans on many points which left some of his companions deeply dismayed because they saw it as a sign of weakness. However, Muhammad showed a deeper understanding of God's way. He was not concerned about appearing to lose face if he could avoid bloodshed and achieve long term gains. In the treaty it was agreed that Muhammad and his pilgrims would return home without entering Mecca, but from now on, Muslims from Medina were free to come to visit the city of Mecca. They could trade with the Meccans, which meant that more normal human relations could be established between the two communities. This led to the conversion of many of the Meccans to Islam and opened the way for Muslims in Mecca to worship openly. These treaty negotiations happened in 628 CE. It was agreed that in 629 CE a group of Muslims could come to Mecca as pilgrims, and the way was opened for Mecca to become a Muslim city from 630 CE onwards. All without the need for battle and the bloodshed that would go with it.

Many Muslim commentators on the Qur'an, have interpreted the verse, 'Indeed we have inaugurated for you a clear victory' (Q. 48:1) to be a reference to the Treaty of Hudaibiyya. It was a great but bloodless victory in the cause of justice, because ancient Arab custom said that all groups of pilgrims had the right to enter Mecca and worship at the Ka'bah. Indeed, it was a greater victory than this, because it restored Mecca to the Muslim community and won many converts to the way of Islam.

What was Hussain to do in the circumstances that he now faced? Bloodshed should be avoided if at all

41

possible, such loss of human life would be a terrible thing. But a far greater tragedy would be the loss of the integrity of the message that had been entrusted to the Muslim community by the Qur'an and the Prophet Muhammad. That must be preserved in its purity at all costs. And so, Hussain resolved to avoid fighting if at all possible, but come what may, to fulfil his destiny of preserving the message of Islam.

7.

TO PLACE ALL ONE'S TRUST IN GOD

We have all been touched deeply by the sight of men, women and children, often in inflatable boats, trying to cross the Mediterranean Sea to seek safety and a new life in Europe. People risk everything on such a dangerous journey to escape war, hunger, or oppression. They trust in a better future; that God will take care of them. We are disgusted when we hear of human traffickers taking money from people in such distress and then breaking all their promises and leaving them in danger of their lives. Just how much can you trust anyone's promises: politicians, rogues, even friends? Sometimes life can be a choice between good and bad, but sometimes it's a choice between bad and something much worse. What is it to trust absolutely? 'In God we trust' but at the end of the day is it not the economy that makes all the difference?

We know that today there are tens of millions of people in the world who have had to leave the place of their birth. They are driven by war, conflict, hunger, and poverty. Some are in search of liberty; some want to find a better future for themselves and for their children. There are many stories that would break the heart of those who hear them.

Hussain also felt the need to leave his home city of Medina. What were the reasons? What motivated him? To be a Muslim is to obey the commands of God and avoid those things that God has forbidden. The source of this knowledge is the ethical guidance contained in the Qur'an and put into practice by the Prophet Muhammad. The tyrant permits the things that God has forbidden and neglects those things that God has commanded. He fails to follow and implement that divine guidance. For the faithful Muslim, not to oppose such tyranny would be to abandon the way of God. The Qur'an commands that faithful men and women are 'to promote the good and to oppose the bad' (Q. 3:110). There is no choice in the matter. Hussain felt himself obliged to make a stand, to do whatever it took, to pay whatever price, to protect and to propagate the purity of the message of Islam. This was the motivation that required him to leave his home in Medina.

Before he left Medina, Hussain wrote his last will and testament and left it with his half-brother, Muhammad ibn Hanafiyya; Ali was the father of both but with different mothers. In this he said, 'Indeed, I have not moved out boisterously, insolently, corruptly or oppressively, rather, I have risen up seeking to put right the affairs of the community of my grandfather, and to act in accordance with the conduct of my grandfather and father.' Muhammad ibn Hanafiyya expressed his concern for what would become of Hussain and his family if they left Medina. He counselled that they should go first to Mecca, but if for some reason they were not safe there, they should travel from place to place including as far as Yemen. Hussain responded, 'If there would not be any shelter or place of refuge in the world, I would never make the oath of allegiance to Yazid.'

Hussain wanted to take his leave of his grandfather Muhammad. He visited his grave, which was in Medina. He wanted to pray there for God's blessing and for guidance. It is reported that he prayed, 'O God, indeed I love the good and hate the forbidden. I beseech you, O Lord of majesty and honour, by the honour of this tomb and the one buried here, provide me with a cause with which you and your prophet are delighted.' It was on this occasion that Muhammad appeared to him in a dream and said, 'O Hussain. Set out on your journey, for God has surely willed to see you as a martyr.' When asked why he was taking the women and children of his family with him, he replied that the Prophet also said to him that God has surely willed to see them taken captive.

After the death of their mother Fatima, Hasan and Hussain were looked after by one of Muhammad's wives called Umm Salama. They were naturally very close. Hussain went to bid farewell to her before he left Medina. She expressed her grave concern at what would happen to him and his family if they fell into the hands of the soldiers of Yazid. Hussain responded by saying, 'I am aware that I shall be slain out of animosity and the Almighty has wanted to see my family members disbursed and my children slain and taken captive, bound by chains, while they are crying and appealing for help but they do not find any helper.'

This statement of Hussain pulls us up short. One can imagine those who heard it from the lips of Hussain himself: 'Did he just say that God wills the death and captivity of his children?' We might share that same thought. Can that be right? Consider the case of someone who has a serious and aggressive cancer that will kill them if it is not treated. The treatment is to infuse into their body poisonous chemicals that are designed to hit the cancerous cells so hard that it kills them, but stops short of killing the person. We have all seen the terrible side-effects of chemotherapy. Only the most serious of illnesses could justify such a devastating treatment.

When Shi'a Muslims consider the events that we

are soon to explore, in which members of the family of Hussain were either killed or taken captive at Karbala, they too are shocked at the severity of the situation. What kind of an 'illness' could justify such a terrible 'treatment'? The situation was of the gravest kind. The way of life founded on the Qur'an and Prophet Muhammad was on the very edge of being subverted by tyranny and base corruption. If the message was lost, humankind would suffer through lack of guidance to lead people to Paradise. The horror of the events had to be experienced by those involved. With the benefit of hindsight, subsequent generations of Shi'a Muslims can grasp the enormity of the loss that alone could justify such terrible sacrifices.

The tragedy of Karbala cannot have been something that did not touch Hussain himself. We see again the enormity of the situation. It is a sign of the total faith and trust that Hussain had in God. He was called willingly to submit to the will of God, even at such a terrible price. He was to light a beacon of faith and submission to God that would blaze through all future generations. The Qur'an recounts the test of faith and submission of Abraham and his son Ishmael (Q. 37:102–106). Abraham was told to sacrifice his son. When Ishmael was told by his father that it is the will of God that he is to be sacrificed, he gave his total submission to God and agreed to be the willing sacrificial victim. In this account, the sacrifice was stopped before Ishmael was killed. In the tragedy of Karbala, the sacrifice runs through to its ultimate conclusion. Hussain and two of his sons are killed. His wife and remaining children are taken captive. The beacon lit by such an act of sacrifice is used by God to light the way of faith and submission for all future generations.

It was in the same month in which Mu'awiya had died and Yazid had taken power that Hussain was to set out on the journey from Medina to Mecca. He knew now that this would be the last time that he would be in Medina and so he wanted to go to the cemetery to bid farewell to his grandmother and his brother. Then he gathered his wife, Rubab, his five children, his sister, Zaynab, and other members of his family, together with some of his most loyal supporters. They were to place their trust in God. They were to set out on a five-day journey riding on camels and horses to go to Mecca. The territory through which they would pass would be hostile; they did not know if they would be intercepted by soldiers. Whatever the hardships, it was the will of God. There was no choice but to obey.

On leaving Medina, Hussain recited from the Qur'an the words that Moses said when he was leaving the court of the pharaoh in Egypt to go to the unknown city of Midian. 'My Lord! Deliver me from the wrong-doing lot' (Q. 28:21). Scholars understand that he was drawing a parallel between Moses setting off on a mission that would save the Israelites from slavery and his own mission to save the message of Islam and its people from tyranny and corruption. The five-day journey of 350 kilometres (220 miles) brought them to Mecca. Upon entering the city, Hussain again recited from the Qur'an a verse attributed to Moses as he turned his face toward Midian, 'Maybe my Lord will show me the right way' (Q. 28:22).

8.

RESPECT FOR HOLY PLACES

One of the great servants of God whose story is told both in the Bible and in the Qur'an is Moses (Musa). Moses has an encounter with God at a burning fire (Exodus 3 and Q. 20:9 and following). In both accounts Moses is told to take off his sandals because the ground on which he stands is holy. This symbol of respecting a holy place by removing one's footwear is commonly found in many religious traditions. The Sacred Mosque in Mecca is indeed one of these holy places for Muslims. Who would desecrate a holy place? Who would not want to spare the innocent from suffering if at all possible? Are not our big decisions made by being consistent with earlier small decisions?

∼

When Hussain, his family, and companions reached Mecca they lived there openly for around four months. During this time Hussain made frequent visits to the Ka'bah. He performed the minor pilgrimage (*umrah*) on several occasions. Many people sought him out to ask his guidance and to enquire what he intended to do when confronted by the tyranny of Yazid.

The agents of Yazid had shown no respect for Medina, the City of the Prophet. They had been willing to attack and kill Hussain there. By moving to Mecca, the City of God, surely there was a hope that they would have some respect and would not offer violence in this holy place. Having respect for holy places, for the people who worship there, and indeed not abusing that which they worship is commanded by the Qur'an. 'Do not abuse those whom they invoke besides God, lest they should abuse God wrongfully without any knowledge' (Q. 6:108). If this degree of consideration is commanded even for those who worship something other than God, surely then Muslims will respect other Muslims in the City of God.

During the time that he was in Medina and in Mecca, Hussain received many letters from the citizens of Kufa in Iraq inviting him to come to them. This had been the power base of his father Ali but their faithfulness was often wavering. This is a topic that we will explore in more depth shortly but it caused Hussain to reflect deeply on what he was called to do next. He knew that at some time there would have to be a showdown with the forces of Yazid. It is reported that he would often recite two verses from the Qur'an in particular during this time.

Fighting has been prescribed for you, even though it is repulsive to you. Yet it may be that you dislike something while it is good for you, and it may be that you love something while it is bad for you, and God knows and you do not know. (Q. 2:216)

Those who have faith fight in the way of God, and those who are faithless fight in the way of the rebel. So, fight the friends of Satan. (Q. 4:76)

Hussain discerned that he was called to journey towards Iraq.

When it became known that Hussain intended to go towards Kufa, some people approached him to dissuade him from this journey. Some tried to persuade him to give the oath of allegiance to Yazid and thus save himself. Others were afraid that he would be killed if he went and so the divinely-appointed leader of the community would be lost. One of these was Hussain's cousin, Abd Allah ibn Abbas. He expressed his concern that the people of Iraq could not be trusted and so advised that Hussain and his family should remain in Mecca. If it was not possible to remain in Mecca then his advice was that Hussain should go to Yemen, where 'There are very strong and fortified castles, as well as high and remote mountains where you can carry out your activities quite away from the reach of the Umayyad government.' Hussain thanked him for his kind advice but said that he was resolved in his decision to go to Iraq. At this Ibn Abbas replied, 'Now that you have decided to depart, please do not take the women and children with you, for I fear that the people of Kufa will kill you in front of them.' Again, Hussain replied that he did not consider any alternative other than taking his family and children with him.

The time for the great annual pilgrimage of the Hajj drew close. Mecca was beginning to fill with a huge gathering of people. Fundamental to the principle of Hajj is that there should be no violence of word or action during these days. It was not allowed even to pluck a flower. Word came to Hussain that Yazid had sent an assassin in the disguise of a pilgrim with orders to kill Hussain wherever he might be found. Such an action would be in complete violation of the spirit of Hajj. Hussain discerned that the time of his departure was drawing very close.

It is reported that Hussain delivered a sermon in Mecca just before the beginning of Hajj. He declared that death is inevitable for all human beings. He made it clear that he knew that he was going to his own death in the coming days. He had discerned that this was the will of God and his decision was to be obedient in all things, and thus to accept death as a martyr as

God so willed. In closing he declared to the gathering, 'Be aware that whoever is willing to sacrifice his blood for us in the cause of God, they must accompany us, for I will set off tomorrow morning, if God so wills.'

Hussain decided to leave Mecca on the first day of the Hajj. This is the day before the standing at Arafat, perhaps the most sacred day of the year for Muslims. It is the day when those on the Hajj remember that all human beings will stand before God on the Day of Judgement. The pilgrims remember the sins of their lives, express their repentance to God and open their hearts to receive God's mercy and forgiveness. We should notice the great seriousness and importance of Hussain leaving the day before this most sacred day. He was determined that the holy city of Mecca, in particular during this most sacred season, should not be defiled by bloodshed. If Hussain had been attacked at this time, there would have been carnage because the assassin had brought an army of men with him and many faithful Muslims would have fought to defend or avenge Hussain. Hussain left Mecca heading into the desert in the direction of Iraq accompanied by the members of his family and his companions who had journeyed with him from Medina. Some additional people joined his party and set out with him.

9.

FICKLE FRIENDS

We often speak about 'fair weather friends'; when things turn bad, they are nowhere to be seen! How many people do you think that you could rely upon when things get tough? Even more of a problem: how many groups could you rely on to stand beside you? If a group had let you down before, would you ever trust them again? Does a bad reputation stick with us forever? What it must be to trust someone completely to check things out for you and give you an honest report! We get a dozen junk e-mails in a day; if you received a hundred, would it persuade you to believe them?

When Iraq came under Muslim rule in 638 CE, the city of Kufa was created to house the garrison. According to Shi'a understanding, Ali was the first divinely-appointed Imam and should have assumed office directly on the death of the Prophet, in the event he came to power only in 656 CE as the fourth caliph, and there was opposition to him from the outset. Ali knew that his duty was to restore the way of Islam to the purity of the original message. This meant reverting to justice in all things, treating everyone equally and making no distinction between Arab and non-Arab. Some of those who had been amongst his closest friends and who had supported his right to leadership did not like the way that he strictly followed the code of Islam. They formed a group who were so strongly opposed to him that they called him to battle. This was the first civil war in the history of Islam. It was a short-lived fight, called the Battle of the Camel. It was fought in Iraq near the city of Basra. It was the army from Kufa that joined forces with Ali to win the day. After this, in 657 CE, Ali moved the capital of the Muslim empire from Medina to Kufa.

The people of Kufa had been the first community outside Medina to pledge their support for Ali. When he arrived in their city he was welcomed by the leading people. He chose a simple house to live in as a sign of the kind of community that he wanted to create. By moving to Kufa, he wanted to spare Medina from future strife. Kufa was more central in the growing empire and from there he was able to keep a closer watch over the governor of Syria, Mu'awiya, who was based in Damascus, but who refused to accept Ali as the head of the community.

One of the fundamental teachings of the Qur'an, as implemented by Prophet Muhammad, was to break the old tribal and clan loyalties which divided society one against another. In an Islamic society, there was the family and there was the whole of the community (the *umma*); there were to be no loyalties in between. This promoted the concept of the equality of all people in Islam. To return to this principle was one of the aims that Ali set himself as head of the community. Some of the people of Kufa greatly favoured this approach. Theirs was a society of many different clans and groupings. Not surprisingly, some clan chiefs in Kufa, especially those who had hung back from supporting Ali in the Battle of the Camel, were not in favour of Ali's approach because they had too much to lose. When it came to fighting against the army of Mu'awiya in 658, at the Battle of Siffin, it was not possible for these clan chiefs to avoid joining with Ali. They were half-hearted and lukewarm in their support. They wanted to withdraw and go home as soon as possible. In this way we can see that the people of Kufa as a whole could not be trusted to stay the course and to honour their word, even though other groups in Kufa, who were committed to the cause of Ali, were fully behind him in the battle.

As soon as it was known that Mu'awiya was dead and that Yazid had been appointed as caliph in breach of the treaty between Hasan and Mu'awiya, some of the leaders of Kufa were keen to put pressure on Hussain to call the Muslims to arms and attack Yazid. They wrote letters to Hussain in Medina and sent them with envoys. 'Now that Mu'awiya has perished, and the Muslims have got rid of him, we find ourselves in need of an Imam and a leader who would rescue us from agitation and anxiety and to lead our wrecked ship to the shore of survival...We are now eagerly waiting for your arrival and shall devote our utmost to support your strategy to attain your aims. We shall not fall short of devoting our properties and lives to your cause.' Such letters arrived frequently in the following months, some from individual leaders in the community, and some with many signatures.

Hussain knew that the people of Kufa could be fickle in their support. He wanted to test how serious they were on this occasion. He sent a cousin of his, Muslim ibn Aqil, to go to visit them in Kufa, gauge the degree of support that could be relied upon, and then to report back to Hussain, so that he could make an informed decision. Muslim ibn Aqil was the son of Ali's older brother, Aqil, he was also married to Ali's half-sister. He had been true to the cause of Ali throughout and therefore Hussain felt that he could trust this member of his extended family with this crucial task.

Hussain knew well that the people of Kufa, like so many who appeared to support him, could not be trusted in their allegiance. He had lived with the Kufans for many years. The example of their conduct towards his father and his brother was always before his eyes. He had nowhere else to go. The many letters that he had received justified him in making Kufa his destination.

10.

WHEN THE GOING GETS TOUGH

Travelling through the desert on camel and horse-back for days on end is no joke. The critical thing is water: one must go from one water source to the next carrying as much as one can. The heat, sand, dust, and thirst respect no-one: men, women, and children, age and station in life make no difference. As an elite military force might say, 'When the going gets tough, the tough get going.' Could we persevere with a cause even when innocent friends and relatives are cruelly treated and killed? Do we then turn back, or is our conviction strong enough to do what we know is right? How do we react when other people decide differently and turn aside from the cause?

∼

When Hussain, his family, his companions from Medina, and some people from Mecca who had decided to join with him, left Mecca on the first day of the Hajj, they headed into the desert to make the gruelling journey to Kufa, in Iraq. They rode on camels and horses but they had to travel light. The women and small children would ride in enclosed shelters on the backs of camels. The swaying of the camels could make even this 'luxury' pretty unpleasant. The youngest child, Abdullah Ali Asghar, was a babe-in-arms, just a few months old. Others in the group were approaching sixty-years-old. They all shared the same conditions and trudged on day after day.

Several incidents are reported when people met them on the journey and learned of the mission of Hussain. They tried to persuade him to turn back, or to turn aside to some other place. Some of these travellers had come from Kufa. One gave a dire warning, saying 'Their hearts are with you but their swords are against you.' A few of those that they met on the journey decided that they would join Hussain's company and go with him.

Muslim ibn Aqil had left to travel to Kufa in the middle of Ramadan 680 CE. When he got there and people learnt of his mission, they thronged to him. Thousands pledged allegiance to Hussain. Some of those who opposed Hussain in Kufa wrote to Yazid in Damascus. They complained that the governor of Kufa was weak and was allowing Muslim ibn Aqil to

win over a great deal of support. Yazid took counsel
from his advisers. Their advice was that he should
send the governor of Basra, Ibn Ziyad, to take over
as governor of Kufa. Ibn Ziyad's father, Ziyad, was
ridiculed because he was illegitimate. Eventually,
Mu'awiya's father, Abu Sufyan, admitted that he was
his father. This meant that Ziyad was proclaimed as
a brother by Mu'awiya, and therefore Ibn Ziyad was
Mu'awiya's nephew, except that Ibn Ziyad was also the
product of an illicit relationship. This put Ibn Ziyad
completely in debt to Mu'awiya; both he and his father
owed their complete social standing to Mu'awiya's
public acceptance of them into his family. Now Yazid
decided to call in the debt and to make Ibn Ziyad his
agent to do his dirty work in Kufa.

Yazid sent Ibn Ziyad to Kufa to undermine the
support for Hussain and to kill Muslim ibn Aqil. Before
he arrived in Kufa, Muslim ibn Aqil was convinced
that a substantial body of the people would stand
firm in the cause of Hussain. He wrote a letter to
Hussain telling him to make haste and come. Ibn
Ziyad had money and power. He used both to bribe
and to threaten people so that they would withdraw
their support for Hussain. Eventually, the supporters
of Muslim ibn Aqil dropped away from thousands,
to hundreds, to just a handful. Now Ibn Ziyad could
make his move; he had him arrested and brought to
the governor's residence. After abusing him, he had
him taken up to the roof and beheaded. His head fell

to the ground and then they threw his body after it. His body was tied to a horse and dragged through the city as a warning to others.

One of the few men of influence who stood by Muslim ibn Aqil and offered him hospitality for some time was Hani ibn Urwa. He was the chief of his clan and was said to have 12,000 men-at-arms. His support was also cut out from underneath him until he too was arrested and brought before Ibn Ziyad. He was an old and highly respected man, but he was beaten and then taken out to be beheaded. Like Muslim ibn Aqil, his body was dragged through the city as a warning.

The heads of these two men were sent by Ibn Ziyad to Yazid in Damascus as proof of their execution, of the governor's grip on power, and to seek the approval of his master. A letter applauding his actions and commending him was received from Yazid. Both men had been betrayed by people in Kufa. A similar fate befell Qays ibn Musahir, a messenger that Hussain had sent to Kufa to tell Muslim ibn Aqil that he was on his way. He too was betrayed to Ibn Ziyad, who had him arrested, and then ordered him publicly to curse Ali and Hussain. When given the opportunity to speak in public he praised these two leaders and publicly cursed Yazid and the Umayyad clan. The governor had him taken up to the roof of his residence and then thrown to his death in the square below.

News eventually reached Hussain in the desert to say that these three followers of his had met their deaths in such cruel ways. It was reported that no army awaited Hussain in Kufa. Indeed, the people had turned against him following the bribes, threats, and brutality of Ibn Ziyad. The invitation for Hussain to go to Kufa was hereby revoked. Hussain called all his company together and gave them the news that the expected welcome and support from Kufa would not be forthcoming. He told them that he released them from any obligation to journey further with him and that those who wished to were free to go home without hindrance. Some members of his company decided to leave. These were people who had joined in Mecca and on the journey; they had been expecting a victory based on the support of the people of Kufa. Those who remained with Hussain and journeyed on with him were his family and close companions who had set out from Medina. Eventually, a handful of men from Kufa would manage to escape the city and join forces with Hussain.

11.

THE POWER OF GOODNESS AND COMPASSION

Which is the greater act of charity: to give away the surplus that you don't really need or to share something that we really need for ourselves? There are different ways of changing the hearts of bad people. One way is to expose them to pure goodness and allow it to have its effect. Do we not have the saying, 'A spoonful of honey attracts more flies than a barrelful of vinegar'? Shakespeare tells us, 'The quality of mercy is not strained'; mercy must be freely given, it cannot be forced. Can human beings be as merciful as God? When is the right time to tell people 'home truths' even though they are unwelcome? When should we keep quiet? What must it be like to receive orders that demand that you do something that you know is not right? How does it grind away within one's heart?

For many hundreds of years sayings attributed to Jesus have circulated amongst Muslims in the Arabic language. Jesus is acknowledged as a prophet in the Qur'an; therefore, it is no wonder that Muslims have always sought wisdom from him. One of these sayings speaks of Jesus walking through the market square when people were abusing him. He always responds to their abuse with a blessing. His disciples become annoyed and ask why he doesn't rebuke those who abuse him. Jesus answers, 'Out of a pure heart only pure words and actions can flow.'

Once Ibn Ziyad had a firm grip on power in Kufa, he sent out an army of men from that city to intercept and shadow Hussain and his companions on their journey. Their leader was a man called Hurr. He was an established and well-regarded army commander from Kufa, noted for his bravery. Hurr was a man of firm belief and piety but not someone involved in politics. He had been recommended to Ibn Ziyad as someone who would execute his orders. Hurr's men met up with the party of Hussain about 70 miles (110 kms) from Kufa. They were hot, dusty, sweating and fatigued from their journey. They entered the camp of Hussain some time before the midday (*zuhr*) prayer. Hussain knew that things were turning against him in Kufa and so was uncertain of the intention of these new arrivals.

He asked them if they had come to join him or to fight against him. At this, Hurr replied that they had not come as friends.

Hussain's reaction to this news was to greet them with words of peace and then order his men to give water to the men from Kufa so that they could drink and wash. Likewise, he said that the horses and camels should be given water to drink and sprayed with water to refresh them. Water is the most precious commodity in the desert. This was water that Hussain's men had drawn the previous day for their own needs on the journey. This was not the welcome that Hurr and his men expected!

The newcomers had a chance to rest before the time for the midday prayer. When the call to prayer was finished, Hussain approached Hurr to invite him and his men to join in the congregational prayer or, if they wished, to pray separately. Hurr responded that he and his men would 'perform the prayer together with you in one line.' In this way both groups formed one congregation for prayer with Hussain acting as the prayer leader. By doing this Hurr and his men had recognised a certain spiritual authority in Hussain.

After the prayer, Hussain addressed the men who had come from Kufa with Hurr. He explained to them that he had been invited by many letters from the people of Kufa and that he was responding to those invitations. Now these men assembled had to decide if they were going to honour those invitations and pledge allegiance to him. It was not his plan to force himself on the people of Kufa. It is reported that Hurr and his men made no response to this speech.

The time came for the afternoon (*asr*) prayer and again the men from Kufa joined the companions of Hussain and prayed behind him as leader. After the prayer, Hussain again addressed Hurr and his army. He made it plain to them that, if they were pious and knowledgeable Muslims, then they would recognise that Hussain, the son of the daughter of Muhammad, had the God-given right to lead the Muslim community. Those who had been failing to live by the teachings of Islam and increasing division and hatred within what should be a united community, by which he meant Yazid and the Umayyads, had no claim to leadership. These men of Kufa had to decide if they were going to be true to their letters of invitation and follow him, or to accept the authority of Yazid and Ibn Ziyad.

Hurr responded by saying that he had never heard about any such letters of invitation. At this Hussain ordered that the letters should be produced. Two bags were brought out, packed with letters from the leaders of Kufa. These were emptied in front of Hurr, who again protested that he had no knowledge of them.

Hussain and Hurr now entered into conversation. Hurr made clear that his mission from Ibn Ziyad was to bring Hussain to him, to stop him turning away in another direction or from returning the way that he had come. Ibn Ziyad's fear was that Hussain would slip through his fingers. Hussain repeated that he was responding to letters of invitation from the people of Kufa. If they had now decided to switch allegiance and desert him, then he was prepared to turn back. To this Hurr replied that he could not allow him to do so; his orders were to bring him to Ibn Ziyad. Hussain replied that no matter how Hurr tried, he would find it almost impossible to bring him to Ibn Ziyad.

When Hussain ordered his party to move off and turn back, Hurr and his men prevented them and some skirmishes took place. The women in Hussain's party were naturally terrified. Hussain addressed Hurr: 'May your mother mourn you! Why are you preventing us from going back?' Hurr had great respect for the Prophet and his family. He replied: 'By God! If any man amongst the Arabs had mentioned my mother, then I would have done the same! But I cannot do so to you since your mother was Fatima.'

Seeing Hussain's resolve and being reluctant to fight him, Hurr suggested a compromise. His original orders required him to bring Hussain to Ibn Ziyad in Kufa, but they did not include fighting him. He suggested that they should journey together away from Medina but take a route that deviated from the straight road to Kufa. During this time Hurr said that he would send a letter to Ibn Ziyad requesting new orders. He concluded, 'I hope that I am saved from a confrontation with you. I remind you, that if you resort to the sword and start a battle, you will certainly be slain.'

Hussain replied, 'Do you frighten me with death? Can you do anything other than kill me?' He then quoted the speech of a man who was leaving his family to go to the help of Prophet Muhammad.

I shall rush towards death, which is not a disgrace for a youth when his intention is right and he fights as a Muslim, when he wishes to support those who do good by sacrificing his life, by disagreeing with the criminals and those who are the enemies of God. I am offering my life and do not wish to retain it, so as to confront a magnificent army in a fierce battle. If I live, I won't regret it; and if I die, I shall not be blamed, while for you, it is enough to live in disgrace.

In the days to come, while Hurr and his men shadowed the party of Hussain in their journey, the words and actions of Hussain had a strong impact in the heart of Hurr. To understand this, we need to jump ahead a little in our story. In Karbala, on the day of the massacre itself, Hurr was lined up with the Umayyad army ready to attack and kill Hussain and his companions. Suddenly, he broke ranks, and rode his horse to stop beside Hussain. He begged his mercy and forgiveness for the part that he had played in leading him to this place of his death. He asked if he might be allowed to join the company of Hussain and to die with him in the cause of right. Hussain forgave him totally and accepted him into his company, so that he could die alongside his companions and thus attain the highest dignity of being a martyr.

We are told that God gave two sayings (*hadith qudsi*) to Muhammad to be proclaimed amongst the people as an indication of the nature of mercy and forgiveness with God. In the first, God said, 'I have taken upon myself the law of mercy; my mercy will overcome my wrath.' In the second, God said, 'If my servant comes to me with sins as high as a mountain but with repentance in his heart seeking forgiveness, he will find it.' The meaning here is that God's mercy has no limits for those who repent and seek to reform their lives. The forgiveness of God does not leave one crippled; rather one is reinstated to the full dignity of a servant of God and thus capable of performing the highest deeds of goodness. The only limiting factor is what is in the heart of the believer. Shi'a Muslims reinforce this understanding by saying that the justice of God demands that God should reward people as God has promised; however, the mercy of God can overwhelm God's justice and God may choose not to punish people according to the just punishment for their sins. As a pure and sinless servant of God, Hussain here sets an example of the quality of mercy which one hopes for from God, and therefore, to which one should strive in human affairs.

12.

'IT IS MY DESTINY'

Think of someone who's just had their first baby; could you ever explain fully just what lies ahead? It's one thing to be filled with excitement going for the first time to an unknown land to help to relieve the people's suffering after a disaster; it's quite another to go subsequent times when you know what lies ahead! Do we have any real freedom in life? Is life all destined, all written for us, we just have to play it out? What does it mean to walk into a future that we have freely chosen but we know will end in our death and the death of those whom we love? Which is the true leader: someone who endures the hardship with the rest of the people, or someone who is sheltered in a palace?

∽

Once Hurr and his men had made contact with the party of Hussain, they did not leave them. The two groups moved on a parallel path so that Hussain was constantly under the watchful eye of the agents of Yazid. Their path diverted from the direction of Kufa and they went further into the desert. Hurr and his party were all seasoned men who could be expected to endure the hardships of a desert journey. In the company of Hussain, in addition to the men, there were also women and children. All had to endure the privations of life in the desert: sparing every drop of water, sleeping in tents, preparing food on open fires, caring for the children and the constant trudging of their camels and horses ever onwards. Hussain shared their lot in every way, but with an acute sensitivity that stemmed from a deeper grasp of what lay ahead.

A model for the present situation can be seen in the action of the Prophet Muhammad when he was willing to commit to mutual cursing, the *mubahala*, as we have already seen in the first chapter. On that occasion he was prepared to take the field with his entire family, the Ahl al-Bayt. Not just his own life was at stake, but also the lives of the future generations of his family, those called to be the divinely-appointed leaders of the Muslim community. Death awaited those who were proved liars by God. Following this model, Hussain has in his company his three sons and two daughters; the entire next generation of his family. Everything that he has is placed at the disposal of God in total trust. The life of faith is not a matter merely of reciting words; it demands that those words are backed up with actions. This total commitment by Hussain should not be seen as a disregard for the lives of his children. We might reflect upon the actions of his father, Ali. It is reported that, at the Battle of Siffin, Ali was concerned about the whereabouts of his two sons, Hasan and Hussain. They represented the line of blood descent from Muhammad and so he was concerned that their lives and that blood line should not be cut off. However, he trusted in God for their preservation in the battle.

To grasp what is happening here, we need to reflect on the meaning of victory for Hussain. We have seen the way in which he has sought to avoid bloodshed on many occasions. We have heard him say that he is not seeking a military confrontation with the people of Kufa. We have noted him saying that whether he lives or whether he dies is not the ultimately important question for him. Since before he left Medina, when he went to bid farewell to his grandfather Muhammad, he has known that he was called to martyrdom. He was told too that his wife and children would either be slain or taken captive. Victory for Hussain is not equated with winning a military battle. Victory is not even preserving his own life; he knows that that will not happen. Victory means, quite simply, total obedience to whatever it is that God wills. Victory means a complete submission of his will to the will of

God. Whatever the apparent price that must be paid is only relevant from the perspective of this world. God is the giver of his life and that of his children; it is for God to decide when and how each life should end. With the benefit of fourteen centuries' hindsight, we can see that the act of total submission, which led to his martyrdom and that of his family and companions at Karbala, was a complete vindication of his stand against injustice and tyranny; a comprehensive victory. It was as though Hussain had a glimpse of the timeless significance of what he was called to do.

Hussain has said that martyrdom is his destiny. Destiny is sometimes spoken of as though it were all written like the script of a play. The actor has no choice about the actions which the character in the play performs. That is a kind of dehumanising view of destiny. One of the unique gifts that God has given to human beings, as Muslims understand it, is the gift of freewill. We are not puppets on strings with God controlling us. Destiny for Hussain is to discern what it is that God wills and then freely to accept it. God is good and only wills what is good; there is no evil in God. Complete surrender to the divine will must necessarily mean that the outcome will be good. It may not appear that way from a human perspective. The tragedy of Karbala remains a tragedy, a massacre, the wilful destruction of innocent human lives. There is no way of escaping the agony through which Hussain, his family, and his companions are going to pass. If we can try to see things from the perspective of God for a moment, as far as we can, then the outcome of this tragedy will be to lay down a marker, a role model for all subsequent peoples; an example of human living in total submission to the will of God.

We can gauge the importance of the mission on which Hussain is embarked from a speech that he made to the men of Kufa who accompanied his party. He quoted a tradition reported from Prophet Muhammad: 'Anybody who sees a tyrant ruler who treats the things that God has prohibited as though they were permitted...And does not revolt against him in words or deeds, God has every right to drive him to the same place as the tyrant [i.e., hell].' Hussain added, 'Be aware that the Umayyads have preferred obeying Satan and have abandoned obeying the all-merciful God. They have supported corruption, failed to implement divine justice and have declared permissible things that have been declared unlawful and forbidden.' Hussain then went on to declare that he was the divinely-appointed head of the community and that they were duty bound to follow him as the letters from Kufa had promised. He called upon them to honour their invitation to him. He reminded them that they had already neglected the allegiance due to Ali and Hasan, and had broken faith with Muslim ibn Aqil. 'Anyone who breaks his pledge does so to his own detriment.' He thus made it clear that the whole reason for the stand that he was taking was to preserve the purity of the message which had been given through the Qur'an. 'I intend to command what is good and prohibit what is evil and to return to the conduct of my grandfather, Prophet Muhammad.' As the leader of the Muslim community he had no other option if he was to remain true to the duty placed upon him.

By undertaking the mission on which he had embarked he was following the example of his father, Ali, who is reported to have said at the Battle of Siffin, which he fought against the forces of Mu'awiya, the father of the current Umayyad ruler, Yazid: 'I also pondered about this war a lot and spent several nights reflecting on it. I found myself at the crossroads of the battle between war and blasphemy, and preferred the war to blasphemy. This is because God will never be satisfied with his servants when a sin is committed on earth and they are silent and remain content with the prevailing situation, and stop encouraging people to do the good and lawful, and forbidding others from committing the forbidden. Hence, I have found battling these people easier than enduring the chains of hell.'

As they continued their journey, some men from Kufa came out to meet with Hussain. They explained that the clan chiefs in Kufa had received bribes and threats from Ibn Ziyad. They told him that a huge army was assembling in order to fight against him. They said that not even one person in Kufa could be relied upon to come to their aid. Already enough men were assembled to defeat Hussain and his companions and yet their number and weapons were constantly increasing. Ibn Ziyad had ordered that every able-bodied man in Kufa must, under pain of death, enlist in his army to take the field against Hussain. The visitors from Kufa pleaded with him to turn aside into the high mountains where he would be safe; there they could draw together other men who would fight alongside him. Hussain thanked them for their concern but said that he would rather continue on his journey. He knew that Yazid would seek him out wherever he went and that he could put a powerful army into the field; the same army that had conquered Egypt, Syria and Persia. The larger the number of men who gathered to Hussain's side, the greater would be the loss of human life. This was not Hussain's intention. He wanted to send a message to all future generations. The dramatic effect of the tragedy that was about to unfold would be heard like a clarion call to touch the hearts of all human beings.

Further on their journey Hussain and his party encountered a man who had fought against Ali at the Battle of Siffin and had a bad reputation for his many criminal acts. Hussain rode into his camp and had a conversation with him. He invited him to repent of his many sins and express that repentance by joining with Hussain in the coming battle. The man explained that he was certain that Hussain and his companions would be killed and that he was very much afraid of death so he would not join with him. He even offered Hussain his horse, which had carried him to victory against all his enemies, so that, if the worst happened, he also could flee from his enemy. Such thoughts of flight were far from the thinking of Hussain! Hussain told him that he had no need of assistance from those who refuse to sacrifice their life for the cause of right. He advised him to go far away from the place where the battle would take place so that he would not hear the cries for help. 'By God! Nobody hears our cries for help and does not come to help us but God will throw them into the fire of hell.' By going to the camp of a known sinner, to invite him to repentance and to atone for his many sins, Hussain was reflecting that willingness of God to grant forgiveness to even the greatest sinner if they should repent and seek that forgiveness.

13.

CORRALLED AT KARBALA

How hard it can be to resist the pressure of the group! Can it ever be right to give in? What about when the bullying tyrant demands that we obey, even though we know it's wrong? Was it really fair to put people on trial at the Nuremberg War Trials? What are the limits of acceptable tactics in war? Can it be right to deprive people of the basic right to water? To starve people into submission? What is it to be a leader when those that one leads are clearly suffering! What about the pressure on parents when they hear their children crying in distress?

❧

After Hurr had sent a message to Ibn Ziyad requesting new orders, the party of Hussain and Hurr's soldiers moved forward, keeping a watchful eye on each other. As he rode, Hussain kept repeating a verse from the Qur'an: 'Surely we come from God and to God we will return' (Q. 2:156). This verse is customarily recited by Muslims when they hear of a death. His eldest son, Ali Akbar heard this and asked him why he was repeating it now. Hussain explained that, while riding on horseback he had fallen into a short sleep, during which he had had a dream in which a horseman appeared saying: 'The people travel and death travels to them.' From this Hussain learnt that death would soon be theirs. Ali Akbar responded, 'May God deter any unfavourable incident. Are we not on the right path?' To which, Hussain replied, 'By God! We do not take any step except on the right path.' This prompted Ali Akbar to say, 'In that case, we do not care about death if we are destined to be slain in the right path.' At this, Hussain blessed him, saying, 'May God reward you with the best of rewards.'

Eventually, a horseman arrived from Kufa and handed a letter to Hurr. The letter was from Ibn Ziyad and read: 'As soon as you read my letter, take Hussain to an uncomfortable place, a place without access to water, which has no defences.' Hurr informed Hussain of his new orders, at which Hussain rebuked him and demanded to be allowed to lodge in one of the nearby villages. Hurr replied that he was no longer free to decide; these were the orders, and the messenger was there to make sure that they were carried out and then to report back.

One of the men in the company of Hussain, Zuhayr, suggested that they should attack Hurr and his men as they were relatively few in number. He knew that a huge army would shortly arrive. Once that happened then the odds against a victory would be impossible. Hussain replied that he would not start the fighting. Again, we can see that Hussain was inspired by the example of his father, Ali. At the Battle of the Camel, the forces against Ali attacked twice and killed a large number of his followers. He ordered his men not to retaliate. Instead he ordered them to have a peaceful dialogue with their enemies in the hope of resolving the matter without further bloodshed.

It was now the second day of the new year according to the Islamic calendar, the second of Muharram 680 CE. Nearby there was a flat plain where Hurr told them to pitch their tents. It is reported that Hussain enquired about the name of this place and some locals gave a couple by which it was known but these did not fit the prophecy about the place of his death. When the name of Karbala was mentioned (*karb* meant sorrow and *bala* meant calamity), Hussain recognised it and said, 'This is the land of sorrow and calamity. Stop here and do not move, put down the luggage, do not depart from here; for by God this is our landing site. By God! This is the place where our blood will be shed. By God! This is the place where our families will be arrested as captives. By God! This will be the location of our tombs. By God! Here is where we will be resurrected. This was what my grandfather, the Prophet of God, promised me.'

After they had pitched camp Hussain again reminded his companions of the reason for their stand against Yazid. The things that are right and good were not being promoted and the things that were wrong and bad were not being opposed. This was the message that he wished to bring to the forefront of their minds at this critical time. He continued, 'I do not consider death except with happiness and living together with the oppressors except with misery. People are slaves of the world and religion is but a liquorice on their tongues, preserved so long as their lives go well; however, when they are subject to examination, the believers decrease in number.'

Hurr wrote to Ibn Ziyad to inform him that they had made camp at Karbala. He received a reply addressed to Hussain: 'I have been informed of your arrival in the region of Karbala, and the Commander of the Faithful, Yazid ibn Mu'awiya, has ordered me not to take any rest, or to be satisfied with food, until I kill you, or you obey my order and pledge allegiance to Yazid.' Hussain threw the letter to the floor. When the messenger told him that a reply was expected, he answered, 'His letter has no reply but the punishment of God.'

The man appointed to lead the Umayyad army on the Field of Karbala was Umar ibn Sa'd. He was someone who owed both his military and his political position, as the Governor of Persia, to the patronage of Ibn Ziyad. We can say therefore, that he was his creature. He arrived at Karbala on the third of Muharram with four thousand men to join with the force commanded by Hurr. This was the vanguard of a much larger force, which was to assemble over the next few days. The initial force comprised professional soldiers who had been diverted from a mission to Persia but those who arrived later were citizens of Kufa, who had been forced to join up. Some of them had managed to escape and flee to hide in villages along the way until the fighting was over. Other men from the surrounding area had likewise been forced to enlist in the army of Ibn Ziyad.

Umar's orders were to contain Hussain and his party at Karbala and to cut off their access to water so as to drive them into submission through thirst. This was achieved by stationing a company of men between the camp of Hussain and the river from which they would draw water. Access was denied from the seventh of Muharram onwards. The suffering in the camp can be imagined: men, women and children in desperate thirst. Mothers unable to quiet the crying of their children!

A handful of faithful followers of Hussain from Kufa came to join his company during these days at Karbala. Hussain gathered together the owners of the land around Karbala and agreed to purchase it. He then endowed it for public use with the request that they should bury the bodies after the massacre that he knew was shortly to happen and that in future they would be willing to direct pilgrims to the place of the graves. The people who buried the bodies of Hussain and his companions belonged to the tribe of Banu Asad.

Hussain sent a message to the camp of Umar to say that he wished to meet him. A tent was set up between the two camps where the two could meet. Hussain addressed him, 'O son of Sa'd! Woe unto you! Do you intend to fight me? Do you not fear God to whom you will return? I am the son of Ali and of the Prophet Muhammad. Do you not want to be with me? This is indeed closer to God, the sublime.' Umar responded by saying that he was anxious about his house in Kufa, that it would be destroyed if he showed disloyalty to the Umayyads. Hussain promised to build him a new house. Then he expressed his anxiety about his garden and date palms. Hussain promised him a better garden. Then Umar said that he was concerned about his family in Kufa, that they might be killed if he refused to obey orders. Finally, Hussain, knowing that they were all feeble excuses, responded, 'May God kill you at your home very soon and not forgive you on the day when you are resurrected.' This encounter probably happened on the eighth of Muharram.

After this encounter, Umar, who was reluctant to fight with Hussain because of his spiritual position, but at the same time, did not want to lose the governorship of Persia, wrote to Ibn Ziyad saying that he thought that Hussain was sincere and that it would be possible to negotiate a solution rather than kill the grandson of the Prophet and members of his family. Hussain would agree to go back and not bring trouble to the people of Kufa. When Ibn Ziyad read this letter, he hesitated and considered such a solution, but his resolve was stiffened by Shimr, one of his advisers. He pointed out to Ibn Ziyad that it would be a grave mistake to let Hussain go now that he had him under his control. Rather he suggested he should demand the oath of allegiance from him, then it would be clear who was the master in the land. Convinced by this advice, he told Shimr that he should go to Umar with a message. If Umar refused to execute his orders, then he, Shimr, was to assume command of the army and do the job himself.

The text of this message, which constituted the final order for the battle at Karbala, read as follows:

I did not send you to Hussain for you to restrain yourself from fighting him, or to idle the time away with him, or to promise him peace and the preservation of his life, or to make excuses for him, or to be an intercessor on his behalf with me. Therefore, see to it that, if Hussain and his followers submit to my authority and surrender, you send them to me in peace. If they refuse, then march against them to fight them and to punish them; for that is what they deserve. If Hussain is killed, make the horses trample on his body, both front and back; for he is a disobedient rebel and I do not consider that this will be in any way wrong after death. It is my view that you should do this to him if you kill him. If you carry out your command concerning him, we will give you the reward due to one who is attentive and obedient. If you refuse, then we withdraw the command of our province and army from you and give the army to Shimr. We have given him our authority.

14.

THE FINAL ULTIMATUM

What courage does it take to face certain death in a cause that is right? Is there something more important than life itself? Not 'something worth living for' but 'something worth dying for'. If there is something worth laying down one's life for, does this make any sense without a belief in life after death? What kind of a leader gives his men a final chance before the battle to save themselves? Is it not more common that the leader will demand that his men stand their ground and face the consequences with him?

When Umar ibn Sa'd read the final orders from Ibn Ziyad, that had been brought by Shimr, he was furious. He said to Shimr, 'Shame on you! May God never show favour to your house. May God make abominable what you have brought to me. By God! I did not think that you would cause Ibn Ziyad to refuse what I had written to him and ruin for us a matter which we hoped to set right. Hussain will not surrender, for there is a spirit like his father's in his body.' Shimr asked him if he was going to carry out the governor's orders or if he was going to hand the command of the army to him. Umar said that he would execute the orders himself.

Shimr then went forward so that he could be heard in the camp of Hussain. Umm al-Banin, who was one of the wives of Ali, came from the same tribe as Shimr. Four of her sons, who were therefore related to Shimr, were present in the company of Hussain. Shimr called them by name and they stepped forward: Abbas, Ja'far, Abd Allah and Uthman. He guaranteed them safe passage if they would leave Hussain. The young men responded, 'God curse you and curse the security which you offer without offering it to the son of the Prophet of God.'

Umar gave orders that his men were to march forward towards the camp of Hussain. This was the ninth of Muharram, soon after the afternoon (asr) prayer. Hussain's sister, Zaynab, heard the approach of the army and went to alert her brother. Hussain had been taking a rest and announced to Zaynab that he had seen Muhammad in a dream. Muhammad had said to him, 'You are coming to us.' Hussain turned to his half-brother, Abbas, and told him to ride out to meet the army and to ask them what they were going to do. He received the response, 'The command of the governor has arrived that we should offer you the opportunity of submitting to his authority otherwise we must attack you.' When Abbas went back and reported this to Hussain, he was told, 'Go back to them, and if you can, delay them until the morning and persuade them to keep from attacking us during the evening. Then, perhaps, we may be able to pray to our Lord during the night to call upon him and seek his forgiveness.' The request was granted with the caution, 'If you surrender, we will send you to our governor, but if you refuse, we will not leave you any longer.'

At night, the company of Hussain gathered round him and he said to them:

> I glorify God with the most perfect glorification and I praise him in happiness and misfortune. O God, I praise you for blessing us with prophethood, teaching us the Qur'an and making us understand the religion. You have given us hearing, sight and hearts, and have made us among those who give thanks to you. I know of no followers more loyal and more virtuous than my followers, nor of any family more pious and more close-knit than my family. May God reward you well on my behalf. Indeed, I do not think that there will be any further days left to us by these men. I permit you to leave me. All of you go away; you are released from your oath to follow me, there will be no further

obligation on you from me. This is a night whose darkness will give you cover. Use it to ride away.

Abbas, the half-brother of Hussain spoke up and was followed by all those of the family: 'We will not leave you to make ourselves continue living after your death. God will never see us do such a thing.' There was a general response from the whole group in the same vein. Hussain then turned to the sons of Muslim ibn Aqil, the cousin of Hussain who had already been martyred for the cause in Kufa. 'Sons of Aqil, enough of your family has been killed. So, go away as I have permitted you.' They replied, 'Glory be to God, what would people say? They would say that we deserted our shaykh, our lord, the sons of our uncle Ali, who was the best of uncles. That we had not shot arrows alongside them, we had not thrust spears alongside them, we had not struck swords alongside them. At such an accusation, we do not know what we would do. No, by God, we will not do such a thing. Rather we will ransom you with our lives, property and families. We will fight for you until we reach your destination. May God make life abominable for us after your death.'

One of the sons of Hussain, Zayn al-Abidin, was sick with a fever and being nursed by his aunt Zaynab. They heard the words of Hussain, who was in his tent reciting a poem, which spoke of his own death and that of his companions on the next day. Zaynab jumped up, tearing at her clothes in anguish and went to him.

She said, 'Then I will lose a brother. Would that death had come to me before today! It is like the day that my mother Fatima was dead, that my father Ali and my brother Hasan were dead.' Hussain said to her, 'O sister don't let Satan take away your forbearance.' Then tears filled his eyes and he said, 'If the desert birds are left alone at night, they will sleep.' In response, she said, 'O my grief, then your life will be violently wrenched from you and that is more wounding to my heart and harsher to my soul.' At this she began to lament, to strike herself and to tear her garments. Then she fainted. Hussain went to her and bathed her face with water. Then he tried to console her by saying, 'O sister, be patient, and know that all living creatures on the earth shall die, those in the heavens will not survive, everything will perish except God, who created the earth with his might and will resurrect the creatures so they will come into being again. God is alone in this regard. My father was better than me, my mother was better than me, my brother was better than me; they all left this world for the world hereafter. For me and for every Muslim there is a perfect example in the Prophet of God.'

Hussain then addressed Zaynab and his other female relatives: his sisters, daughter, and wife. 'O my sister! O Umm Kulthum! O Fatima! O Rubab! Pay attention to me; when I am killed, you must not tear your clothes, nor strike your face, nor cry out with grief and loss.'

Hussain then ordered that the tents should be moved closer together so that it would not be possible to ride through them. A trench was to be dug at both sides and the back of the tents and filled with wood that could be set on fire to prevent a surprise attack from the rear. This way any attack must come from the front.

Hussain withdrew to his tent and spent the night in prayer, in reciting the Qur'an, in making supplications to God and seeking God's forgiveness. Likewise, his followers did the same. One of the verses of the Qur'an that Hussain is reported to have recited on this night is as follows: 'Let the faithless not suppose that the respite that we grant them is good for their souls: we give them respite only that they may increase in sin, and there is a humiliating punishment for them. God will not leave the faithful in your present state, until he has separated the bad ones from the good' (Q. 3:178–9).

These verses of the Qur'an set the tone for the day that was to follow. The apparent victory in battle of the forces of the Umayyads: Yazid, Ibn Ziyad, Umar and Shimr, will be a short-lived thing. It will encourage them to sink further into depravity and indeed their final punishment will be all the more awesome. The forces of godliness, of truth, justice, and uprightness will be put to the test, as are all peoples, and although Hussain and his companions will be slain, the victory of submission to the will of God and upholding a cause that is just will act as an example to all future generations.

15.

EVERYTHING IS COMMITTED
– *TO THE LAST DROP OF BLOOD*

What would it take for you to be willing to sacrifice your life for a cause? What kind of people continue to volunteer for battle and certain death when they have seen their companions, young and old, brutally massacred? What burden is on the heart of a leader who is asked to give permission to such people to go to their deaths when they volunteer? What about when such men and boys are not just companions and volunteers but sons, brothers and nephews? What does this say about commitment, the significance of the cause and the belief that, ultimately, they will be vindicated?

❧

Everyone in the camp of Hussain was awake and

alert with the first signs of daylight on the tenth of Muharram 680 CE, the Day of Ashura. They all assembled for the morning prayer (*fajr*) and afterwards Hussain gathered them all together. He was surrounded by seventy-two male companions, armed and ready to face an army of around thirty thousand men. Notwithstanding their small number, Hussain assigned them to their places with left and right flanks, and the tents, containing the women and children, to their rear. He ordered that the wood in the ditch to the rear and both sides of the camp should be set on fire to prevent any attack other than to the front of his men.

Umar ibn Sa'd assembled his men, gave them their formation for battle and assigned commanders to each division. When the cavalry began to approach, Hussain raised his hands in prayer: 'O God, it is you in whom I trust amidst all grief. You are my hope amidst all violence. You are my refuge and provision in everything that happens to me. How many grievances: the heart may weaken in it, the means may disappear in it, a friend may desert me in it, and the enemy may rejoice in it. I lay it before you and complain of it to you, because of my desire for you alone. You relieved me of it and removed it from me. You are the master of all grace, the possessor of all goodness and the ultimate resort of all desire.'

Shimr, the man who strengthened the resolve of Ibn Ziyad and challenged Umar to turn over the command of the army to him, came forward to taunt Hussain and his men. One of Hussain's archers asked permission to take a shot at him and hopefully kill him. Hussain refused him permission, saying, 'I am unwilling to begin the fighting against them.'

Hussain addressed the army assembled against him:

O people of Iraq! Listen to my speech and do not make haste until I have given you a piece of advice concerning your duty towards me, and I make clear the reason for my coming here. If you accept my explanation, verify my truthfulness and deal with me with justice, you will attain prosperity, and then there would remain no way for you to fight me. And if you reject my explanation, denying my reason and do not make a fair judgement, 'Then conspire together, along with your partners, leaving nothing vague in your plan, then carry it out against me without giving me any respite' (Q. 10:71). 'My guardian is indeed God who has sent down the Book, and God takes care of the righteous' (Q. 7:196).

O People! Reflect upon who I am, then look to yourselves and question your thought processes. Do you think it is lawful for you to kill me and to violate my sanctity? Am I not the son of your Prophet's daughter, the son of the trustee of the Prophet and his cousin [Ali], who was the first believer in God, and the first to embrace what his Prophet had brought from his

Lord? Has not the statement of the Prophet of God regarding me and my brother reached you, 'These two are the Princes of the Youths of Paradise'? If you do not accept what I have stated is the truth – and it is indeed the truth, for by God, I have never told a lie since I realised that God hates whoever tells a lie and shall defeat the liar – then there are indeed among you some people whom, if you asked, could inform you of this and they will report to you, for they have heard this statement about me and my brother from the Prophet of God. Is this not sufficient to prevent you from shedding my blood?

Hence if you are still in doubt regarding this statement, do you doubt that I am the son of your Prophet's daughter? By God! Between east and west in the world there is no son of the daughter of a prophet except me. Woe to you! Do you want me in revenge for a slain individual I have killed, for a property I have damaged, or for a wound I have inflicted?

At this stage, Hussain called out to four of the leading men of Kufa, who had written to invite him to come to them and who were present, 'Did you not write to me, "The fruits have ripened, the region has become verdant, and you will arrive to find an army ready for you"?'

They replied, 'We do not know what you are talking about!'

Then one of the four called out, 'Submit to the authority of your kinsmen (the Umayyads). They have never treated you with anything but what you liked.'

Hussain responded, 'No! By God! I shall never give them my hand in humiliation to make a compromise and shall not evade them in the way slaves do. O Servants of God! "Indeed, I seek the protection of my Lord from every arrogant one who does not believe in the Day of Reckoning" (Q. 40:27).'

Hussain then continued to address the assembled army in general:

Behold! The illegitimate one, son of the illegitimate one [Ibn Ziyad], has pressed me between two choices, war and abasement. And how far is abasement from us! God does not like to see that in us, nor his Prophet, nor the believers. Surely, our chaste mothers, and those with dignified spirits, and the valiant souls of our fathers do not allow us to choose the obedience of the abased over the honourable death of noble men. Be aware that I have informed and warned you! Be aware that I am prepared to fight you with this family of mine, in spite of the small number of my companions and the desertion of those earlier supporters.

'Indeed, I have put my trust in God, my Lord and your Lord. There is no living being but God holds it by its forelock' (Q. 11:56).

O God! Deny them rain, give them years such as the harsh years of Joseph, and put in charge of them the ruthless Thaqafid youth [a brutal ruler who came to power only fifteen years later], who will make them quench their thirst with a cup of bitterness where none of them would be left unpunished. O God! They have told us a lie and abandoned us. 'You God are our Lord, we place our trust in you, and to you do we return' (Q. 60:4).

When Hussain had finished speaking the army made to advance against his camp. At this point Hurr, the commander of the men who had accompanied Hussain's party through the desert and had forced them to camp in a land without water, whom we have already encountered, was humbled by Hussain's speech. He went to Umar ibn Sa'd and enquired if he really intended to fight Hussain. He replied firmly that he did. Hurr, feeling subdued and miserable, broke ranks and rode towards Hussain's camp and pleaded forgiveness from him. Hussain readily forgave him and welcomed him to his camp. Observing the lack of water in the camp and the thirsty lips and frightened faces of the women and children, Hurr took his stand in front of Hussain's men to address his former comrades and fellow citizens.

People of Kufa, may your mothers be deprived of their sons and tears come to their eyes. Have you summoned this righteous man to come to you, then, when he has come to you, have you handed him over to his enemies? Did you claim that you would fight with your own lives for him, and then have you begun to attack him in order to kill him? You have laid hold of his life; you have seized his throat; you have encircled him on every side in order to prevent him returning to God's broad land, from which he came. He has come into your hands like a prisoner who no longer has the power to use his own life and cannot defend it against harm. You have prevented him, his womenfolk, his children and his people from getting the water of the Euphrates to drink. They are likely to die of thirst. How wickedly have you treated the offspring left by Muhammad! May God not give you water to drink on the Day of Thirst.

At this Umar put an arrow to his bow and shot it in the direction of Hussain and his men. He cried out, 'All of you bear witness to who was the first to shoot.' At this there was a general exchange of archery. Then, as was the custom, one after the other, champions of both sides came forward for single-handed combat. But the men of Yazid's army were no match for the valiant and brave-hearted volunteers of Hussain's camp, who victoriously overpowered and killed their opponents. One of the divisional commanders of the Umayyad army realised that such single combat was futile because the champions from Hussain's company were pleased to fight to the death and thus to seek martyrdom. He called for a change of tactics. There followed a general attack by foot-soldiers, archers and cavalry. The men of Hussain's company, although greatly outnumbered, continued to give a good account of themselves but many of them met their deaths. They ranged in age from an old man of around seventy-five years to youths, some of whom had barely reached puberty. Some were high-born and many were servants, who had performed their duties to Hussain and his family. Hussain would habitually give them their freedom before they entered the field of battle so that there was no question but that martyrdom was their free choice.

On several occasions it was noted that Hussain would rush into the field of battle to bring comfort to men mortally wounded and to strengthen them in their dying moments. The words that Hussain spoke were a mixture of the assurance of Paradise and comfort and strength in their final agony. Hussain did not differentiate according to the class from which each came; there are no class divisions on the field of martyrdom. We read of him going to his dying Turkish-speaking servant, embracing him and putting his cheek on his face. Such a gesture greatly touched the dying man. One further example can be taken from the case of Jawn, a dark-skinned servant, who had experienced racial prejudice in the past. When he came to Hussain to ask for permission to go to the battlefield, Hussain responded, 'O Jawn, you are free to leave me because you have followed us in the quest for comfort, hence do not get yourself into trouble in our cause.' At this it is recorded that Jawn threw himself at the feet of Hussain to appeal: 'O grandson of the Prophet of God! Is it fair that I used to be dependent on your favour in your time of comfort and convenience and leave you alone when you are in trouble in front of the enemy? No, by God! I will never part with you until my blood mixes with your fragrant blood.' At this Hussain gave him permission to go to fight, and as he lay dying Hussain went to him and prayed, 'O God! Lighten his face, perfume him, resurrect him with the nobles, and acquaint him with Prophet Muhammad and the Family of the Prophet.'

The fierce fighting continued until almost midday. When the time came for the midday (*zuhr*) prayer, Hussain sent a message to request a cease-fire so that the prayer could be offered. This was declined. Nevertheless, Hussain and his men assembled for the prayer in spite of a rain of arrows. Some of those who remained of Hussain's party took station in front of him so that he would not be shot with an arrow while at prayer.

Then five hundred archers drew up in ranks and fired salvos of arrows at the men and horses of Hussain. A great many men and horses were wounded. This was followed by fierce fighting on foot. The way in which the companions of Hussain fought, their fearlessness and dedication in the face of an overwhelming army, and the manner of their deaths had an impact on some of the opposing army. One noted archer decided to change sides, took station in front of the tents of Hussain and wreaked havoc on his former comrades with his deadly bow. At one point, Hussain called out, 'Isn't there anyone to help us? Isn't there anyone to sacrifice his life in favour of the families of the Prophet of God?' It is reported that two brothers, who fought with the Umayyad army, were so touched by these words and by the impact that they had on the women and children in the camp of Hussain, that they decided to change sides and rushed to the camp of Hussain. They fought with great valour and both died as martyrs in the cause of justice and truth.

The companions of Hussain, who were not related to him by blood, came to him, one after the other, to seek permission to go forward to meet their deaths in battle. They had pledged not to allow any harm to come to the Family of the Prophet so long as they were alive. Eventually, only the members of the Family of the Prophet remained to stand beside Hussain. There now stepped forward Ali Akbar, the eldest son of Hussain, who was noted for his likeness to Muhammad, both in looks and in his character. It is said that people who had never met the Prophet but wanted to gaze upon him would seek permission to look at Ali Akbar on account of his close resemblance. He went to bid farewell to his father and seek permission to go forward.

Hussain gave him permission, but as he was departing, Hussain raised his eyes to the heavens, and said, 'O God! Bear witness concerning this group of people [the Umayyad army] towards whom a youth has gone out bearing the closest resemblance to your Prophet Muhammad in creation, manner, and speech such that when we yearn to look at your Prophet we cast a look at him.' As Ali Akbar was going forward to fight, Hussain addressed directly Umar ibn Sa'd: 'What happened to you? May God break your kinship ties as you have broken your kinship ties with me; you have not considered my blood relationship with the Prophet of God.' The enemy were reluctant to attack Ali Akbar on account of his resemblance to Muhammad. Eventually, he was confronted by a group of men and mortally wounded, having been weakened more by thirst than fighting. As he lay dying, he called out to his father, 'O father! Now my ancestor, the Prophet of God, has just quenched my thirst with a cup of water from Paradise after which there will never be any thirst.' Hussain rushed towards him and gazed at his mutilated body, before exclaiming, 'May God annihilate the people who have slain you. O my dear son! What has made them so forgetful about God as to offend the sanctity of the Prophet of God. May the world be made dust after you.' At this Zaynab, the sister of Hussain, came running out and threw herself on the dead body of her nephew. Hussain raised her up and led her back to the tent. He told some members of his family to carry their brother's body back to the tent.

Ali Akbar was the first of seventeen martyrs related to Hussain to die that day. Zaynab's own sons, called Aoun and Muhammad, were both killed. Three of the sons of Aqil, Ali's older brother, met their deaths at Karbala and two of his grandsons. Three of the sons of Hussain's brother, Hasan, were amongst the martyrs of Karbala. One of them, Qasim, presented a letter to Hussain written by the boy's father: 'My dear son Qasim, when your uncle Hussain is besieged by his enemies from all sides and when every true lover of God and the holy Prophet lays down his life defending the cause of truth, you sacrifice yourself for the cause on my behalf.' At this, Hussain hugged him and both uncle and nephew cried for some time before Hussain allowed him to go to meet his death. The youngest son was Abdullah, who ran to defend his uncle Hussain when he had fallen from his horse and was cut down by a swordsman while so engaged. Five sons of Hussain's father, Ali, also died as martyrs that day, including Abbas, the standard-bearer of Hussain's company.

The youngest child to die that day was the infant son of Hussain, Abdullah Ali Asghar. He was only six-months-old and still at his mother's breast, but owing to the way in which the company had been deprived of water, his mother's milk had dried up and so she was unable to feed him. Hussain took him in his arms to comfort him and sat with him outside the tent. One of the enemy archers let fly an arrow that struck the baby in the neck and killed him. Hussain attempted in vain to stop the bleeding and in so doing his hands were filled with the baby's blood. He was so moved that he threw the blood towards the sky and said, 'O God! What makes all my afflictions easy is that it is happening before your eyes.' Hussain carried his body to lay it beside the other martyrs in the tent set aside for that purpose.

Abbas, the half-brother of Hussain, a noted warrior, worthy in this regard to be likened to his father, Ali, was the standard-bearer for Hussain's company and always to be seen rallying his men to the fight. As the battle wore on and the thirst of the remaining company was extreme, Hussain asked him to make a dash for the river with the view to bringing back a flask of water for the women and children. His attempt was spotted by some of the opposing cavalry who engaged him in mortal combat until he too was killed. Hussain saw him fall and rushed to his side saying, 'Now my back is broken, my means are diminished and my enemies rejoice.' He then expressed his contempt for those who had killed him: 'With your wickedness, O People, you have acted cruelly and expressed hostility to us and to Prophet Muhammad. Did not the best person recommend us to you? Was not my grandfather Muhammad the best person? Was not Fatima my mother? And my father, Ali the Guided? You have been cursed and will be punished for the crime you have committed!'

On the Day of Ashura, Hussain made two important farewells. First, he bade farewell to his wife and other female members of the family. He advised them to put on their outer travelling cloaks and to prepare themselves, 'Get ready for the calamity and know that God is indeed your support and preserver, God will rescue you from the evil of the enemy and make the end of your affair toward the good. He will punish your enemy in different ways, and will grant you in compensation for this calamity various types of blessings and honour; therefore, never complain or express what might harm your status.' Second, he went to his son Zayn al-Abidin, who was still sick with fever and too weak to take part in the fighting. He was to succeed Hussain as the head of the community and it was one of the last duties that Hussain had to pass on his divine appointment, to inform him on matters that were held secretly by the Imams of the community, and to give him wise counsel. In keeping with the tradition passed on from Muhammad, through Ali and Hasan, that the leaders of the community should always have a particular care for the poor and those in need of support, he said, 'O my dear son! I advise you a statement which my father gave me when approaching death, that he received in turn from his father. Never commit any crime against the person who has no supporter except God.'

When Hussain finally stood alone against the army that had come to kill him, he already bore upon his body various injuries to his throat and head. He mounted his horse, armed himself and set off to engage them to the death. He was but one against the remaining tens of thousands of the Umayyad army, yet his resolve was not diminished. At a certain point in the fighting a group from the army decided that they would make an attack against the tents containing the women and children of Hussain's company. Hussain called out to them, 'If you do not have any faith whatsoever and are not scared of the resurrection, at least act with dignity in your life.' At this Shimr, who was with this group asked Hussain what he meant. Hussain replied, 'I am the one who is fighting you, and you have decided to kill me; the women have done nothing wrong, so prevent your men from attacking my family so long as I live.' Shimr replied, 'You do have this right, O son of Fatima!' He then turned to his men and said, 'Stop rushing toward the camp of this man; attack him. Indeed, he is a noble combatant!'

The fighting continued but the men of the Umayyad army held back from pressing their attack out of fear and respect for the grandson of Muhammad. Who could be the one to deal him a mortal blow? Shimr shouted encouragement to the men, both cavalry and foot-soldiers; he ordered them not to hold back but to rush Hussain altogether. This they did and he was struck with sword and spear. He fell bleeding to the ground and with his final strength he whispered his last two prayers (in part):

O God, you are close to the one who calls you. Judge between us and our people, for they betrayed us and fought against us, while we are the family and the descendants of your Prophet Muhammad.

O Lord! To me there is no Lord except you and no one deserves to be worshipped save you! I am patient with your decision. Judge between me and them, for you are the best of all judges.

In the name of God, through the help of God, in the cause of God, and on the path of the religion of the Prophet of God.

At this Hussain died.

16.

WHOEVER SAID THAT WOMEN ARE THE WEAKER SEX?

In recent decades many military forces across the world have included women in equivalent positions alongside men, taking the same risks, enduring the same physical privations, and facing the same dangers. In traditional societies women's roles have been clearly differentiated in time of war, but this by no means suggests that they have shown less courage or strength. How many women, in all ages and cultures, have faced the challenge of sending off their menfolk to war? What must it be to be present at a battle, to dress and arm husbands, brothers, and sons and to send them off to fight? What courage to wait in prayer for their eventual return! And then to receive back their mangled bodies! Suffering hunger, thirst, and bombardment must be terrible for anyone; what about the double burden on a mother whose children are subjected to these horrors of war? And after the battle is ended and lost; what anguish of heart for the women in the camp not knowing how they might be abused by the victors?

The Bible tells us about a mother and her seven sons who were to be tortured until they would agree to eat forbidden swine flesh (2 Maccabees 7). Each brother was tortured to death in turn in the sight of his mother and the remaining brothers. The mother spoke to each son as he was suffering, steeling his courage and begging him not to abandon his faith but to endure to the point of death and martyrdom. All seven brothers remained true to the law of God and died as martyrs; eventually the mother died too.

From the time of the Qur'an and the Prophet Muhammad the situation of women in Arabian society was fundamentally improved. They had legal status in their own right; they were able to profess their faith and convert to Islam without seeking permission from any male relative. Indeed, it was often women who converted first and their influence brought men to faith afterwards. The first Muslim martyr was a woman, who refused to give up her faith in spite of torture from her family. After Muhammad and his community migrated to Medina, when they faced a series of battles against the idol-worshippers of Mecca, who sought to destroy them, the women had their own station in battle. They steeled the courage of the fighting men, tended to the wounded, took care of necessary provisions, and even on occasion, when things got really tough, they took part in the fighting themselves.

The women in the company of Hussain have not been as visible as the men during the story thus far. Often the focus has been on negotiations, threats and the battle itself. However, from the moment that Hussain decided to leave Medina and travel to Mecca, the women of his company were integrally involved. They had to prepare and plan family matters, take care of the children and endure the hardships of the journey and uncertainty about what lay ahead. That first part of the journey was as nothing compared with travelling through the desert from Mecca to Karbala. They endured the hardships of the journey equally as much as the men of the company, but with the additional burden of providing for the children. Once their water supply was cut off the pressure on them increased dramatically. They had to deal with sickness and comfort the children who suffered from thirst. Which mother's heart is not burdened by the thought of crying children, suffering from a thirst about which they can do nothing?

We have seen the anguish of Hussain's sister,

Zaynab, as the awesome reality became clear, that Hussain and all the men of the company were bound to die. We are told that there were eight mothers present at Karbala who witnessed their sons going to fight and being horribly butchered. The courage of these women was surely remarkable: to send off one or more son to give his life in the cause of justice and truth, to honour and esteem his courage, and then to spend the time whilst he was fighting in prayer back at base camp. To be killed in such fighting leaves a battered, torn and often mutilated corpse. As the martyrs were brought back to the camp their bodies were laid out by the women and then what courage they showed to send more men into the battle.

What was it that inspired such acts of courage and dedication? The women of Hussain's company were committed with their menfolk to the belief that Hussain was the rightful head of the community. They believed that tyranny and injustice must be opposed; even at such an awesome price. They had faith in the religion brought by the Qur'an and implemented by Muhammad. For these women it was not any ordinary courage but one based on the strength of their faith and their complete submission to the will of God, no less than that of the men. Their hope and trust were in the vindication of God, into whose hands their lives and those of their menfolk were entrusted.

One of those citizens of Kufa who joined the company of Hussain was Abd Allah ibn Umayr. He was accompanied by his wife and mother. On the field of Karbala, he went to join in the fighting, was badly injured, captured, tortured and died. His wife, who had witnessed his fighting and death, ran out from the tents to embrace his dead body. She wiped off the blood and dust from his face and said, 'Enjoy Paradise! I beg God who has granted you Paradise to make me your companion there!' At this, Shimr ordered one of his men to attack her. He split open her head and she collapsed, dead, over the body of her husband. She is recorded as the only woman martyr on that day. Abd Allah's head was cut off and thrown towards the tents. His mother picked it up, wiped off the blood and dust and then launched herself at the enemy with a tent pole. It was only when she was ordered to return to the tents by Hussain himself that she obediently broke off the engagement.

One of the men of the company of Hussain who was killed in the early part of the fighting was Junada al-Ansari. Later his eleven-year-old son Umar came to Hussain to request permission to join in the battle. Hussain recognised that this young man had already lost his father and questioned whether his mother might be opposed to his joining in the fighting. To this Umar replied, 'My mother ordered me to sacrifice my life in your favour.' At this Hussain gave him permission to join in the fight. He was killed, his head was cut off and thrown back towards the tents. His mother ran and collected it, wiped off the dust, and threw it back at the enemy where it struck a soldier. At that Umar's mother picked up a stake and ran to take part in the fighting herself. Having injured two of the enemy, she was ordered by Hussain to return to the tents.

In addition to Zaynab, the sister of Hussain, who lost two sons at Karbala, and the two mothers about whom we have just read, Hussain's own wife Rubab had to endure witnessing the death of her six-month-old baby shot with an arrow in his father's arms. Both mothers of the sons of Hasan, Hussain's brother, were present to witness their deaths. Another daughter of Ali, Ruqaya, was present to witness the death of her son Abdallah. Finally, another mother, whose name has not been recorded, but who was the mother of Muhammad, a grandson of Ali's older brother, Aqil, had to witness the small boy, clinging to a tent pole, being killed in front of her by one of the enemy soldiers.

We have seen the way in which Hussain went to strengthen and comfort the women of his company at various times during the journey and on the Day of Ashura. We have seen him bid them farewell and counsel them to faith and trust in God in the calamity that would befall them after the battle. They had no way of knowing what they would have to endure. And then they witnessed the final scene of the death of their beloved leader, Hussain.

17.

DEGRADATION BUT THE MESSAGE LIVES ON

Look at refugee camps and the number of displaced people in the world today; so often women and children are over-represented there. The humiliation and degradation that follow war affect women and children the most. How helpless must one feel to be taken captive and to face an uncertain future? How deeply must one believe in a cause to be willing to remain defiant in the face of the victorious enemy? Such faithful witness can touch the hearts even of brutes! It was women who bore and nurtured the martyrs: how often is it the faith of women that keeps the martyrs' message alive? One cannot know the future but one must persevere in a cause that one knows to be right. Could the medical researcher Alexander Fleming ever have guessed the importance of penicillin over the last century? Consider Thomas Guy, whom people spoke of as a miser and yet he was saving to endow Guy's Hospital for the poor of London!

∽

After Hussain was dead his head was cut off. It was displayed as though a trophy of war to the Umayyad army and as a symbol of the utmost humiliation and despair for the women and children who remained of Hussain's company. The body of Hussain was plundered for mementos of the one who had been defeated and killed. Men ablaze with the fire of battle went to pillage the tents of Hussain's camp and to terrorise the women. Cloaks were torn from them and they clung together in dread of what might happen next. There were even those amongst the soldiers who wanted to attack and kill the one surviving son of Hussain, Zayn al-Abidin, who lay wracked with fever in the tent. When Umar ibn Sa'd reached the tents, he put a stop to the looting, ordered that the women should be respected and that Zayn al-Abidin should not be harmed. He placed guards outside the women's tents to ensure that his orders were obeyed. We can deduce that, as the commander of the army, he was ashamed that his men had treated women and children in this way.

Volunteers were sought to make their horses trample over the body of Hussain, both front and back. It is a fundamental Islamic principle in warfare that bodies of the dead should not be mutilated and yet the body of Hussain was broken and pulped under the horses' hooves. A detachment was dispatched to carry the severed head of Hussain to Ibn Ziyad in Kufa as proof that the deed had been done. All the other dead bodies of the companions and family of Hussain were also beheaded. Their heads were distributed amongst leaders of the various clans represented in the Umayyad army as a way of sharing in the responsibility for, and the honour of, the killing of these men. Likewise, these heads were dispatched, mounted on spears, to be paraded through the streets of Kufa and taken to the palace of Ibn Ziyad.

True to their agreement with Hussain, the men of Banu Asad buried the body of Hussain where he fell. His two sons were buried at his feet and the bodies of the other companions and members of his family were buried close to the grave of Hussain. Only Abbas, who had died in a valiant attempt to bring water to relieve the suffering of the women and children, was buried a little distance away where he had fallen.

The next day the women and children and Zayn al-Abidin were bound and transported in triumph to Kufa. They were taken to the governor's palace where the heads of Hussain and the other martyrs were already on display. All the citizens of Kufa were summoned to attend the palace, to view the severed heads and to learn the lesson of what happened to those who opposed the might of Yazid. When the citizens had assembled, Ibn Ziyad began to mock the head of Hussain. He took a cane and poked the teeth with it. At this an old man in the crowd objected strongly. He proclaimed that often he had seen the Prophet Muhammad kiss the lips of Hussain and they should not now be disrespected in this way. He was told that only his old age saved him from the most severe punishment and he removed himself from that gathering immediately. The realisation of what the men of Kufa had been involved in caused considerable shame and dismay amongst many.

At this time the captives from Karbala were brought into the courtyard of the governor's palace. Zaynab, the sister of Hussain, made herself inconspicuous and went to sit in a corner. Nevertheless, Ibn Ziyad noticed her and enquired as to her identity. She made no response but one of the women who accompanied her spoke up and said, 'This is Zaynab, daughter of Fatima, the daughter of the Messenger of God, may God bless him and grant him peace.' Realising that she was the daughter of Ali, at one time the caliph of the Muslims with the seat of his caliphate in Kufa, Ibn Ziyad said in response, 'Praise be to God who has disgraced you, killed you and revealed the false nature of your claims.'

Zaynab immediately retorted, 'Praise be to God who has favoured us with his Prophet, and has purified us completely from sin. He only disgraces the great sinner and reveals the false nature of the profligate. Such men are not among us, praise be to God.'

'How do you consider God has treated your family?' asked Ibn Ziyad.

To which Zaynab replied, 'I didn't see anything but the favour of God. I saw people for whom God had decreed martyrdom and they went forward bravely to their resting places. God will gather you and us together. You will plead your excuses to God and we will be your adversaries before God.'

Anger flared in the heart of Ibn Ziyad but he was restrained by some people in the assembly. He told Zaynab, 'God has healed my soul from the rebel Hussain and the disobedient ones from amongst your family.'

Zaynab cried out, 'By my life, you have killed the head of the clan of the Hashemites, you have pierced my family, you have cut down my young branches and you have pulled out my root. If this heals you, then you have been healed.'

The attention of Ibn Ziyad was drawn to Zayn al-Abidin and he was asked to give his name. He replied with his family name, Ali ibn Hussain. The governor queried, 'Didn't God kill Ali ibn Hussain?'

'I had a brother who was also called Ali and the people killed him', replied Zayn al-Abidin.

'Rather God killed him', affirmed Ibn Ziyad.

This provoked the answer, quoting from the Qur'an, 'God takes the souls at the time of their death' (Q. 39:42). Followed by, 'No soul may die except by God's leave, at an appointed time' (Q. 3:145).

Again, Ibn Ziyad flew into a rage, 'How dare you answer me like that! That answer will be the end of you. Take him away and cut off his head!'

At this Zaynab clung to Zayn al-Abidin and said, 'O Ibn Ziyad, haven't you had enough of our blood? By God, I will not leave him. If you kill him, kill me with him.'

Looking from one to the other, Ibn Ziyad said, 'How strange is this family relationship! I think she wants me to kill her with him. Leave him, for I see that this illness will finish him off.'

Ibn Ziyad now left the palace and went to the mosque. He ascended the raised platform (*minbar*). He praised and glorified God, then said, 'Praise be to God who has revealed the truth and the followers of the truth, and has given victory to the Commander of the Faithful, Yazid, and his party and has killed the liar who is the son of a liar and his followers.' At this the head of an important clan in Kufa who was present stood in front of Ibn Ziyad and the assembly and shouted, 'O enemy of God, you are the liar and your father and the man who appointed you and his father. You killed the sons of prophets and take the place of men of truth on the minbar.' Ibn Ziyad ordered his immediate arrest, but the clan chief gave voice to the battle cry of his clan and immediately seven hundred of his men gathered around him and took him away to safety. That night Ibn Ziyad had him arrested in his house, executed and then his body was crucified and exhibited in public as a warning.

The next morning the head of Hussain, mounted on a spear, was paraded through the streets of Kufa. After this was finished all the severed heads were assembled and the journey began to take them to Yazid in Damascus. The captives were likewise assembled and bound in preparation for the journey ahead of them. Zayn al-Abidin was secured with an iron chain around his neck. The captives soon caught up with the men transporting the severed heads. The journey from Kufa to Damascus took a few weeks because they called at every settlement on the way to display the severed heads and to allow people to see the bound captives. The whole tenor of this exercise was to humiliate and denigrate the survivors and the martyrs of Karbala, and to demonstrate what happens to those who oppose the rule of Yazid.

Eventually, the party comprising severed heads, captives and their guards reached Damascus and entered the presence of Yazid. The head of Hussain was placed on a dish and set before Yazid, who gazed upon it. He then recited a poem: 'The clan of the Prophet [the Hashemites] just sought a kingdom. No revelation was sent to them or any news from heaven...I wish my grandfathers, who were killed in the Battle of Badr [by Ali], could now witness the misery of those who helped the Prophet. Were they present now, they would exclaim with joy applauding my deed.'

He then spoke to Zayn al-Abidin, saying, 'Son of

Hussain, your father cut the bond of kinship with me and showed ignorance of my right, trying to deprive me of my position of authority. Now God has treated him in the way that you have seen.'

Zayn al-Abidin responded by quoting a verse of the Qur'an, 'No affliction visits the earth or yourselves but it is in a book before we bring it about, that is indeed easy for God' (Q. 57:22).

Yazid countered him with another verse from the Qur'an, 'Whatever affliction that may visit you is because of what your hands have earned, though God excuses many an offence' (Q. 42:30).

The captive women and children were arrayed before Yazid and made to sit down. All eyes were on them, some with pity and shame and others gloating or apprehensive. Fatima al-Sughra, the daughter of Hussain, who was aged around nine-years-old, reported that a Syrian man looked at her and asked Yazid if he could have her. She clung to her aunt, Zaynab, who spoke out boldly addressing the man, 'By God, you are a liar. By God, you are too lowly-born! Such a thing is not for you nor for him [Yazid] to decide.'

Yazid reacted angrily, 'You are a liar. That is for me to decide. If I wish to do anything, I can do it.'

Zaynab retorted, 'No, by God! God would not let you do that unless you had left our faith and professed belief in another religion.'

'It is me whom you are treating in this way!'

screamed Yazid, 'It is your father who has left the religion, and your brother.'

To this Zaynab replied, 'It is by the religion of my father and my brother that you, your father and grandfather are guided if you are a Muslim.'

'Enemy of God, you lie!' he shouted.

Zaynab answered him, 'You are a commander, yet you vilify people unjustly and you have oppressed them with your authority.'

At this Yazid remained silent.

Yazid then ordered that the captives should be taken away and held securely. He realised the enormity of the actions carried out on his orders and feared the consequences. Yazid decided to send the captives back to Medina, according them all due respect, to try to save his face. They remained in Damascus for several days. The captives were then issued with new clothes and a guard was appointed to escort them safely back to Medina. The captives requested their guards to allow them to pass by the graves of the martyrs of Karbala, which they did. They paid their respects there and this is the origin of the tradition amongst Shi'a Muslims to this day to make visitations to the graves of Hussain and the martyrs in Karbala, especially on Arbaeen, the fortieth day after the commemoration of the massacre, the Day of Ashura. They then continued their journey back to Medina. The news of the massacre reached Medina before they did and there was great lamentation, which was renewed when the captives arrived.

18.

WHAT IS IT 'TO REMEMBER'?

The Islamic calendar is a lunar calendar, this means that each month is timed around the cycles of the moon; a new moon means a new month. A lunar month is technically twenty-nine-and-a-half days long, but in practice it is either twenty-nine or thirty days long. At the end of the twenty-ninth day one goes out to try to sight the crescent moon; if it can be sighted, then tomorrow is the first day of the new month, and if it cannot be sighted, then tomorrow will be the thirtieth day of this month and the next day will automatically be the first of the new month. There are twelve lunar months in a year, which means that each lunar year is 354 days long; that makes it eleven days shorter than a solar year. Everything timed according to this lunar calendar appears to occur about eleven days earlier every year, when timed according to the solar calendar. The events of Karbala took place in the opening days of the first month of the year according to the Islamic calendar. The first ten days of this month, called Muharram, every year are marked by the remembrance of the events that we have been exploring, culminating on the tenth of that month, the day of the massacre itself, the Day of Ashura.

Why do people need to remember those events every year? If it were merely a question of learning the history and understanding the personalities involved, then once we had done that, there would be no need to do it again. If it were merely a case of being aware of the geography of Karbala, then once people had visited once and seen the shrines and paid their respects to the martyrs buried there, then there would be no reason to go again. To remember the events associated with the martyrdom of Hussain and his companions is much more than a question of history, stories, or geography. So why do Shi'a Muslims place so much emphasis on these ten days, meeting every night to hear again the events leading up to the massacre and indeed, with great sorrow and emotion, reliving that memory?

We could ask why do we remember and celebrate any event every year? Whether it be a wedding anniversary, a birthday or perhaps the anniversary of the death of a member of our family. Especially when we think of someone who has died, we might say that we remember them at this time to keep their memory alive; so that we do not forget the important part that they played in our lives. We might say that they live on in our memory. This is common to all our human experience, but when we move into a religious way of thinking, there is another important step to be made. To grasp what is happening here in a religious context we need to explore more fully the concept of remembering.

From a human perspective, we might count back to the year in which the events took place. We can say that the massacre of Karbala took place on the tenth of Muharram 680 CE. That is to locate it in a human dimension. To understand the importance of a great religious event like the Day of Ashura we need to try to move out of our human, restricted dimension, to see things from God's perspective. This is really difficult because we are creatures, we were born at a certain time, in a certain place; we live, and then we will die at a certain time and a certain place. We humans are limited by time and space. I am alive today not a thousand years ago. I live in this country not on the other side of the world. This is not how things look from God's perspective.

When Muslims speak about God, they say that God is eternal; that means that God is not limited by time at all. God never had a beginning and God never will have an end. God is not old or young; such concepts of time mean nothing from God's perspective. From our human perspective, we have a past tense to speak about history and a future tense to speak about what is yet to come. From God's perspective, there is no time, therefore it is meaningless to speak about the past or the future because everything is present to God 'now'. We call this the 'eternal present' of God.

We humans are physical beings, we have a body and therefore we are fixed in space. I am here and not there. When Muslims speak of God, God has no physical body. Therefore, God is not limited by space. To speak of God in space is meaningless; God is both everywhere and nowhere in our human terms. This means that any event in our creation, wherever it takes place in the universe, is immediately present to God.

If we apply God's perspective to the events of Karbala, then we can say that those events are happening now, at this moment, because there is no time with God. Similarly, we can say that Karbala is not a physical place located in Iraq, but from God's perspective, Karbala is right here and everywhere. This is not an easy concept for us to grasp because we are so used to working in time and space. Indeed, we have another problem; when we try to talk about these things or to explain them, we have to use human language and human concepts, and are bound by the limits of our human perspective. We can only do the best that we can. Our human language and concepts do not penetrate through into God's perspective but they are all that we have to try to talk about such things. You might well have heard the expression *Allahu akbar* used in Muslim circles. It is often translated 'God is the greatest', that is, as a superlative. We might remember a famous heavyweight boxer who used to say often 'I am the greatest' but that only held true until he was beaten! The expression *Allahu akbar* is not a superlative but a comparative, so it would be better to translate it 'God is greater than...' God is greater than anything we can imagine, than anything we can speak about, whether in poetry or in philosophy, greater than anything that we can tie down with our human concepts. So, whatever we can say about God, or God's perspective, it is only the very best that we can manage and 'God is greater than...any attempt that we can make'.

When Muslims remember a great event like the massacre of Karbala, they are seeking to move out from a human perspective and to attempt to see it in God's perspective. This is to move beyond the limitations of our human history into something beyond that: we can call it meta-history. To remember something in meta-history is to make it present here and now. That's what it means to liberate an event from time and space, to lift it from our human perspective and history into God's perspective or God's meta-history. This is the meaning of a phrase that is often used in this context, 'Every day is Ashura and every place is Karbala'.

This has a profound impact on Shi'a Muslims when they remember the events of Karbala. It is lifted out of time and place and made present wherever they are in the world when this time of year comes round. But more than that, because it is lifted into meta-history, the lessons, the example, and the devotion are made present at every moment of every day and in every place and context of daily life. Those examples of total faith, trust, and submission to the will of God that have been dominant themes during our study must be allowed to shape and colour the life and context of every Shi'a Muslim in all times and places. The demand not to submit to tyranny and injustice, to resist them with all one's might, and indeed with one's life, wherever they are encountered, at work, in society, within families or communities, in public and in private life, must become part of the natural disposition for those who follow the example of Hussain and his companions.

By remembering, by making present, the events of Karbala, we can see that these ten days are a time of profound spiritual reflection and renewal in the lives of Shi'a Muslims. The temptations to tyranny and injustice, in small things as well as great, are present in the lives of all human beings in every age and society. So, part of the spiritual discipline during these days of Muharram is to examine and root out those negative elements that have crept into each one's life. We could think of this as identifying elements in our lower human nature that need to be corrected and elevating ourselves to be more like Hussain. By making present once again the exemplary character, not just of Hussain, but also of the companions who embraced death alongside him rather than give in to tyranny, and also the women and children who survived and carried on the message of Hussain after the massacre, an ideal is held up before our eyes of the heights or ideals of which human beings are capable and which can inspire people up until today. The very name Hussain itself means 'one of beautiful character', therefore he is the supreme example for Muslims to live by.

To grasp the significance of this example we need to consider the position that Hussain holds in the understanding of Shi'a Muslims. The Qur'an speaks of certain people as being chosen and purified by God to the ultimate degree. These are those who are of the highest spiritual excellence and as close to God as any human being can be in this life. Such people are extremely rare in human history and the Qur'an mentions Abraham, Moses, Jesus and Muhammad as examples. For Shi'a Muslims Hussain stands in the same company. For such exalted people there is no scope for any base motives in their lives: no selfishness, arrogance or egoism. Their lives are so aligned with the divine that the will of God becomes their will and the word of God becomes their word. When we see Hussain in this light, then we can understand why Shi'a Muslims, as well as many Sunnis, will want to remember his pain, suffering and sacrifice, to be moved to tears by that remembrance, and thus, by loving those who were loved by God, to draw closer to God themselves. By doing so they show their willingness to take on for themselves that perpetual battle for justice, goodness and truth. It is as though their love for Hussain, expressed through their tears of sorrow, will cleanse their hearts and ennoble their characters so that they might be worthy followers of Hussain in this life and companions of his in the life of Paradise.

It is important to reflect again on the meaning of victory in this story. Victory in business might mean a bigger profit or an expansion of the firm. Victory in charitable giving might mean relieving suffering or improving the lot of those in need. How can a story in which the hero and his companions end up being brutally massacred and the women and children taken off as captives represent a victory? In a human perspective, that does not make sense, but in God's perspective, victory is not winning or losing a battle but rather striving for the heights of spiritual excellence, which means that one is prepared to submit oneself totally to the divine will 'come what may'. The victory of Hussain was not about defeating an enemy in battle but rather defeating tyranny that cloaked itself in the guise of religion. It was about defeating the misuse of authority and egoism in the name of God. This is the victory of goodness and truth, because God is the Good and the True. Therefore, removing all that is bad and false in one's life is the highest imitation of the example of Hussain and the greatest striving for closeness to God. This is the victory for which Hussain strove and which he won.

Great religious figures do not belong to the particular community in which they lived and who are charged with keeping their memory alive. Great religious figures belong to God and, as Muslims understand it, God has no favourites; God is not the property of any particular people or religion. Throughout human history God has been guiding humankind on the right path. Therefore, the life and example of a great religious figure like Hussain are not confined to any one faith community. Hussain's influence and inspiration have touched the lives of many people who do not belong to the Muslim community. These are great human virtues that can inspire goodness, uprightness, justice and perseverance for everyone. A relatively small group of people in an obscure desert plain can light a beacon to summon people to promote what is good in every society and to oppose those things that are unjust in every society. Their example is one of the victory of goodness and truth in the face of overwhelming odds. That example can inspire human beings today and people as yet unborn can benefit from our right actions just as we can benefit from the example of Karbala.

Works Consulted

Aghaie, Kamran Scot, *The Martyrs of Karbala: Shi'i Symbols and Rituals in Modern Iran*, Seattle: University of Washington Press, 2004.

Albodairi, M. Ali, *Understanding Karbala: Abridged and Adapted from the original work of the Grand Ayatollah Sayyid Muhammad Saeed al-Hakeem*, The Mainstay Foundation, 2017.

Albodairi, M. Ali, *The Saga: The Sermons of the Ahl ul-Bayt*, The Mainstay Foundation, 2018.

Albodairi, M. Ali, *The Saga: The Battle of Karbala*, The Mainstay Foundation, 2018.

Ali, Mir Ahmed, *Saving Monotheism in the Sands of Karbala*, New York: Tahrike Tarsile Qur'an, 2009.

Ayoub, Mahmoud, *Redemptive Suffering in Islam: A Study in the Devotional Aspects of Ashura in Twelver Shi'ism*, The Hague: Mouton Publishers, 1978.

Chamseddine, M. Mahdi, *Hussain's Revolution: Its Causes and Implications*, The Mainstay Foundation, 2015.

Chamseddine, M. Mahdi, *The Victors of Imam Hussain*, The Mainstay Foundation, 2015.

Chamseddine, M. Mahdi, *An Introduction to Popular Conscience: Hussain's Revolution*, The Mainstay Foundation, 2018.

al-Hakeem, Ali, *Imam Hussain: Life and Legacy*, The Mainstay Foundation, 2019.

Ja'fari, M. T., *Imam Hussain: The Martyr of the Pioneer Culture of Mankind*, Iran: Allameh Ja'fari Institute, 2018.

al-Majlisi, M. Baqir, *Behar al-Anwar*, vols. 44 & 45, New York: The Islamic Seminary, 2014.

Malekpour, Jamshid, *The Islamic Drama*, London: Frank Cass, 2004.

Milani, Fadhel, *Islamic Theology*, London: Islam in English Press, 2016.

al-Mufid, Shaykh, *Kitab al-Irshad (The Book of Guidance)*, London: Muhammadi Trust, 1981.

Najmi, Muhammad-Sadiq, *From Medina to Karbala in the Words of Imam al-Husayn*, Birmingham: Sun Behind the Cloud Publications, 2012.

Naqvi, Ali Naqi, *The Martyr for Mankind* (An Abridgement), London: Muhammadi Trust, 1986.

Pinault, David, *Horse of Karbala: Muslim Devotional Life in India*, London: Palgrave, 2001.

Rizvi, Saeed Akhtar, *Understanding Kerbala*, Iran: Ansariyan Publications, 2006.

Sambhli, Atiqur Rahman, *Hussein's Martyrdom in Historical Perspective*, London: Furqan Publications, 2009.

Shams al-Din, M. Mehdi, *The Rising of Al Husayn: Its Impact on the Consciousness of Muslim Society*, London: Muhammadi Trust, 1985.

Shirazi, Muhammad, *Husayn: The Sacrifice for Mankind*, London: Fountain Books, 2002.

al-Tabari, *The History of al-Tabari*, vol. 16, *The Community Divided*, New York: SUNY, 1997.

al-Tabari, *The History of al-Tabari*, vol. 17, *The First Civil War*, New York: SUNY, 1996.

al-Tabari, *The History of al-Tabari*, vol. 18, *Between the Civil Wars: The Caliphate of Mu'awiyah*, New York: SUNY, 1987.

al-Tabari, *The History of al-Tabari*, vol. 19, *The Caliphate of Yazid b. Mu'awiyah*, New York: SUNY, 1990.